MONETIZE YOUR CONTENT

A comprehensive guide to AdSense for content creators with strategies, tips and best practices to optimize your earnings

TERESA MILLER

TABLE OF CONTENTS

INTRODUCTION

In the vast landscape of digital creativity, where ideas spark and stories come to life, content creators thrive on their ability to captivate audiences and share compelling narratives. Yet, amidst this creative journey, a crucial question arises: how can these creators transform their passion into a sustainable income stream?

Enter AdSense; the beacon that illuminates the path to monetization for online content creators. At its essence, AdSense is Google's ingenious advertising platform designed to empower creators like you to monetize your digital content effectively.

Imagine this: You've crafted a stunning blog post, shot a captivating video, or designed a visually immersive website. AdSense steps in as your monetization partner, seamlessly integrating relevant advertisements into your content. These advertisements, tailored to your audience's interests, appear strategically, complementing your work without disrupting the user experience.

Here's the magic: when visitors engage with these ads through clicks or impressions, you earn revenue. It's a symbiotic relationship—your content draws an audience, and AdSense ensures you earn a fair reward for the value you provide.

But AdSense is not just about plastering ads randomly across your platform. It's a sophisticated toolset offering customization options, analytics insights, and optimization strategies. You can fine-tune the ad formats, choose optimal placements, and access performance metrics to maximize your earning potential.

AdSense doesn't just benefit content creators; it also serves advertisers seeking a platform to showcase their offerings to the right audience. It's a win-win scenario where advertisers reach their target demographic, audiences discover relevant products or services, and content creators monetize their hard work.

However, it's not merely about slapping ads everywhere. AdSense thrives on a delicate balance—a harmony between captivating content and unobtrusive, strategically placed advertisements. It respects the user experience while rewarding the creator for their efforts.

As the digital landscape evolves, AdSense adapts, offering new formats, insights, and policies to ensure fair play and user satisfaction. Navigating this dynamic ecosystem requires understanding its nuances, complying with its guidelines, and harnessing its potential to craft a successful monetization strategy.

Throughout this guide, we'll delve deeper into the intricacies of AdSense, exploring its functionalities, best practices, policy guidelines, and optimization strategies. By the end, you'll be equipped not only to monetize your content effectively but also to strike that perfect balance between captivating your audience and harnessing the power of AdSense.

So, are you ready to embark on this journey, turning your passion for content creation into a rewarding endeavor? Let's unravel the secrets of AdSense together and unleash the full potential of your digital creativity.

CHAPTER ONE

WHAT IS ADSENSE?

AdSense is an advertising program developed by Google that enables website owners, content creators, and publishers to monetize their online content by displaying targeted ads on their platforms. It's a way for individuals and businesses to earn revenue from their websites, blogs, YouTube channels, apps, or other digital properties by allowing Google to place advertisements that are relevant to their audience.

The core concept of AdSense involves advertisers bidding in an auction-based system to display their ads on websites or other online spaces. Advertisers bid on ad space, and Google's algorithms determine the most relevant ads to display based on the content of the site, the user's interests, and other factors.

Here's how AdSense generally works:

• Content Integration: Website owners or content creators sign up for AdSense and embed a piece of code provided by Google onto their web pages, videos, or apps.

• Ad Display: Google's technology scans the content of the pages to understand their theme and context. Relevant ads are then displayed based on this content and users' interests.

• User Interaction: When visitors interact with the ads by clicking on them or viewing them (in the case of impression-based ads), the content creator earns revenue.

• Revenue Sharing: The revenue generated comes from advertisers who pay Google to display their ads. Google then shares a portion of this revenue with the website owner or content creator.

AdSense offers various ad formats such as display ads (text, image, rich media), video ads (on YouTube and other video platforms), native ads (seamlessly integrated into the content), and more. The program provides tools and analytics that allow content creators to optimize their ad placements, track performance, and maximize their earning potential.

However, it's essential to comply with AdSense policies regarding content quality, user experience, and ad placement to ensure continued participation in the program. Violations of these policies could lead to warnings, temporary suspensions, or even permanent bans from the AdSense program.

Overall, AdSense serves as a means for content creators and publishers to generate revenue by leveraging the advertising capabilities of the Google network while offering relevant and engaging ads to their audience.

AdSense, developed by Google, operates as an advertising platform that enables website owners, content creators, and publishers to earn revenue by displaying targeted ads on their online properties. Here's a detailed explanation of how AdSense works:

1. Sign Up and Integration:

• Account Creation: Content creators sign up for AdSense by creating an account through the AdSense website.

• Integration of Ad Code: After approval, they receive a piece of code (AdSense code) from Google. This code is inserted into the HTML of their web pages, YouTube videos, apps, or other digital content platforms.

2. Ad Auction and Contextual Targeting:

• Auction-based System: Advertisers bid in an auction to display their ads on websites or other online spaces. This bidding process occurs in real-time through Google's ad auction system known as AdWords.

• Contextual Relevance: Google's technology scans the content of the pages where the AdSense code is implemented. It analyzes the content's theme, keywords, user behavior, and other factors to determine relevance.

3. Ad Display and User Interaction:

• Display of Relevant Ads: AdSense selects and displays relevant ads based on the content of the web pages or the context of the user's browsing history and preferences.

• User Interaction: Visitors interact with the ads by clicking on them or viewing them (in the case of impression-based ads). These interactions generate revenue for the content creator.

4. Revenue Generation and Payment:

• Revenue Sharing: The revenue generated comes from advertisers who pay Google for displaying their ads. Google shares a portion of this revenue with the content creator or website owner.

• Payment Cycles: Google has payment thresholds, and once the earnings reach a certain amount, typically $100, they issue payments to the content creator via various payment methods like direct deposit, wire transfer, or checks.

5. Tools and Optimization:

• Performance Tracking: AdSense provides tools and analytics to track Ad performance, click-through rates, earnings, and other relevant metrics.

• Optimization Strategies: Content creators can optimize their ad placements, experiment with different ad formats, positions, and sizes, and use the provided analytics to enhance their revenue potential.

6. Compliance and Policy Adherence:

• AdSense Policies: Content creators need to adhere to AdSense policies regarding content quality, user experience, and ad placement. Violations may lead to warnings, temporary suspensions, or account termination.

In essence, AdSense serves as an intermediary between advertisers and content creators, facilitating the display of relevant ads to the right audience, generating revenue for content creators, and providing advertisers access to their target demographic. The success of AdSense lies in its ability to balance user experience, content relevance, and revenue generation for all parties involved.

THE ADVANTAGES OF USING ADSENSE FOR MONETIZING CONTENT

Using AdSense for monetizing content offers several advantages for content creators and website owners. Here are some key advantages:

• Ease of Use: AdSense is relatively easy to set up and integrate into websites, blogs, videos, and apps. Google provides clear instructions and tools to implement ads seamlessly, making it accessible for beginners and experienced users alike.

• Monetization Options: AdSense offers various ad formats such as display ads, video ads, native ads, and more. This diversity allows content creators to choose the most suitable ad types for their audience and platform.

• Access to a Vast Network of Advertisers: AdSense connects content creators with a vast network of advertisers who bid to display their ads. This increases the likelihood of displaying relevant ads that resonate with the audience, leading to higher engagement and potential earnings.

• Revenue Potential: Content creators can earn revenue based on user interactions with ads, such as clicks or impressions. As the traffic to the website or content increases, so does the potential for earning revenue through AdSense.

• Customization and Optimization: AdSense provides tools and features that allow content creators to customize ad placements, sizes, styles, and formats. Additionally, it offers optimization insights and analytics to improve ad performance and maximize revenue.

• Supports Various Platforms: AdSense is versatile and supports multiple platforms, including websites, blogs, YouTube channels, mobile apps, and more. This flexibility enables creators to monetize various types of digital content.

• Global Reach and Targeting: AdSense has a global reach, enabling content creators to monetize their content worldwide. Moreover, its targeting capabilities allow advertisers to display ads relevant to users' interests and demographics, enhancing user engagement.

• Timely Payments: Google has a reliable payment system, issuing payments to content creators on a monthly basis once they reach the payment threshold, usually $100. Various payment methods are available for convenience.

• No Upfront Cost: Using AdSense does not involve any upfront costs for content creators. They can join the program for free and start earning revenue as their content attracts visitors and ad interactions.

• Compliance and Policy Support: AdSense provides clear guidelines and policies for content quality, ad placements, and user experience. Adhering to these policies ensures a sustainable partnership with AdSense without risking account suspension.

Overall, AdSense offers content creators a convenient, scalable, and potentially lucrative way to monetize their digital content by leveraging the power of advertising while maintaining a positive user experience for their audience.

BENEFITS OF ADSENSE FOR CONTENT CREATORS

AdSense offers a range of benefits to content creators, making it a popular choice for monetizing online content:

• Monetization Opportunities: AdSense provides content creators with a straightforward way to generate revenue from their digital properties such as websites, blogs, videos, and apps. It allows them to earn money by displaying targeted ads to their audience.

• User-Friendly Integration: Google offers easy-to-use tools and a user-friendly interface that simplifies the integration of ads into various types of content. The process of setting up AdSense and embedding ads can be done quickly, even for beginners.

• Diverse Ad Formats: AdSense offers a wide range of ad formats including display ads, text ads, video ads, native ads, and more. This diversity allows content creators to choose the most suitable ad types that align with their content and audience preferences.

• Access to a Broad Advertiser Network: AdSense connects content creators with a vast network of advertisers, increasing the chances of displaying relevant ads to the audience. This diverse advertiser base contributes to higher engagement and potential revenue.

• Potential for High Earnings: As traffic to the content increases, so does the potential for higher earnings. Content creators can earn revenue through various monetization models such as pay-per-click (PPC) or cost-per-impression (CPM), depending on user interactions with ads.

• Customization and Optimization Tools: AdSense provides tools and features for customization and optimization of ad placements, sizes, styles, and formats. Content creators can experiment with different configurations to maximize revenue while ensuring a positive user experience.

• Global Monetization: AdSense allows content creators to monetize their content globally. It supports multiple languages and currencies, enabling creators to reach audiences worldwide and earn revenue from diverse regions.

• Insights and Analytics: AdSense offers comprehensive analytics and reporting tools that provide valuable insights into ad performance, user behavior, click-through rates, and earnings. This data helps creators make informed decisions to optimize ad revenue.

• Regular and Reliable Payments: Google ensures timely and reliable payments to content creators. Once the earnings reach the payment threshold, usually $100, Google issues payments through various convenient payment methods.

• Compliance and Support: AdSense provides clear policies and guidelines regarding ad placements, content quality, and user experience. Adhering to these policies ensures a sustainable partnership with AdSense, and support is available for queries or issues.

In summary, AdSense empowers content creators by offering a convenient and scalable platform to monetize their digital content while providing access to a wide array of ad formats, a global network of advertisers, customization options, analytics, and reliable earnings potential.

STEP-BY-STEP GUIDE TO CREATING AN ADSENSE ACCOUNT

Creating an AdSense account involves several steps to get started with monetizing your content. Here's a detailed step-by-step guide:

Step 1: Check Eligibility

Before starting the AdSense account creation process, ensure that you meet the eligibility criteria set by Google:

• You must have a website, blog, YouTube channel, or app where you can display ads.

• Your content must comply with AdSense policies regarding content quality, copyright, and other guidelines.

• You should be of the required age (usually 18 years old) or have parental consent if under the age limit.

Step 2: Prepare Your Content Platform

Make sure your website, blog, YouTube channel, or app is ready for AdSense approval:

• Create high-quality, original content that complies with AdSense policies.

• Ensure your website has important pages like About, Contact, and Privacy Policy.

• Avoid content that violates AdSense policies, such as copyrighted material, adult content, or illegal content.

Step 3: Sign Up for AdSense

• Visit the AdSense Website: Go to the AdSense sign-up page: AdSense Sign-Up.

• Create a Google Account (if needed): If you don't have a Google account, create one. If you already have a Google account, sign in using those credentials.

Start the Application Process:

• Click on "Sign up now" or "Get started" on the AdSense homepage.

• Enter the URL of the site or platform where you want to display ads. Select the content language and your country.

Enter Your Details:

• Fill in your contact information, including name, address, email, phone number, and payment details.

Agree to the Terms and Conditions:

• Read and agree to the AdSense terms and conditions.

Submit Your Application:

• Click on "Create account" or "Submit" to send your application to Google for review.

Step 4: Wait for Review and Approval

• Google will review your application, which may take a few days to several weeks, depending on various factors such as the volume of applications, your website's readiness, and adherence to policies.

Step 5: AdSense Account Activation

• Once your application is approved, you'll receive an email notification from Google. Follow the instructions in the email to activate your AdSense account.

Step 6: Generate Ad Code and Implement Ads

• Access Your AdSense Account: Log in to your AdSense account using your Google credentials.

• Create Ad Units: Generate ad code by creating ad units. Choose ad types, sizes, and styles that fit your website or content platform.

• Implement Ad Code: Copy the generated ad code and paste it into the HTML source code of your website, blog, YouTube channel, or app where you want ads to appear. Ensure proper placement for better visibility and user experience.

• Wait for Ads to Start Displaying: It may take some time for ads to start displaying on your platform after implementing the code.

Step 7: Monitor Performance

• Once ads are live, use the AdSense dashboard to monitor ad performance, track earnings, analyze user interactions, and optimize ad placements to maximize revenue.

Step 8: Receive Payments

• When your earnings reach the payment threshold (usually $100), Google will issue payments based on your preferred payment method.

Remember, it's crucial to adhere to AdSense policies to maintain a healthy account status and continue monetizing your content effectively.

THE ELIGIBILITY REQUIREMENTS AND NECESSARY INFORMATION

To create an AdSense account and start monetizing your content, you need to meet certain eligibility requirements and provide specific information. Here's a breakdown:

Eligibility Requirements:

• Content Ownership: You must own the content or have the necessary rights to display ads on your platform (website, blog, YouTube channel, app, etc.).

• Minimum Age: You need to be at least 18 years old. If you are under 18, you may still apply with parental consent.

• Content Quality: Your content must comply with AdSense policies, which include:

• Original and high-quality content: Ensure your content is not plagiarized, misleading, or infringing on copyright.

• Avoid prohibited content: AdSense does not allow content related to illegal activities, adult content, violence, drugs, gambling, or hate speech.

• Traffic and Visitors: While there is no specific traffic requirement to apply for AdSense, having a reasonable amount of traffic and engaged visitors on your platform can improve your chances of approval.

Necessary Information:

When applying for an AdSense account, you'll need to provide the following information:

Personal Details:

• Name: Your legal name or the name associated with the payment method.

• Address: Your physical address for verification purposes and payment delivery.

• Email: An active email address associated with your Google account.

Website or Platform Information:

• URL: The URL of the website, blog, YouTube channel, app, or other digital platform where you intend to display ads.

• Language: The primary language used on your platform.

• Content Category: The general category of your content (e.g., technology, lifestyle, finance).

Payment Information:

• Payment Address: Details regarding where you want to receive payments, including address and currency preferences.

• Payment Method: Choose your preferred payment method (e.g., bank transfer, check, wire transfer) for receiving earnings.

Tax Information (if applicable):

• Tax Identification Number (TIN): If required in your country for tax purposes, you'll need to provide this information.

Verification and Contact Information:

• Phone Number: A valid phone number for verification purposes and contact if needed.

• Contact Preferences: Indicate your preferred method of contact from Google.

Ensure that the information provided is accurate and matches the details of your content platform to facilitate the approval process. Google will review the information and content quality before approving your AdSense application.

Remember to regularly review AdSense policies and guidelines to ensure ongoing compliance, which is crucial for maintaining your AdSense account in good standing.

Content creators aiming to qualify for AdSense need to fulfill specific criteria set by Google. Here are the key criteria that content creators typically need to meet to be eligible for AdSense:

• Original Content: Content creators should provide original and valuable content that adheres to Google's policies. This content can be in various formats such as articles, videos, images, or apps. It's essential to avoid copyright infringement and ensure that the content adds value to users.

• Content Platform Ownership: You need to own the content or have the necessary rights to display ads on the platform where you intend to use AdSense. This can include websites, blogs, YouTube channels, mobile apps, or other digital properties.

• Compliance with Policies: Adherence to AdSense policies is crucial. Content should comply with Google's program policies, which include guidelines on content quality, prohibited content (like adult content, copyrighted material, violence, illegal activities, etc.), and user experience.

• Age Requirement: To apply for an AdSense account, you must be at least 18 years old. If you're under 18, you can still apply with parental consent and supervision.

• Sufficient Content Volume: While there's no specific requirement for the amount of content, having a decent volume of high-quality content can improve your chances of approval. Ensure that your content provides value and engages your audience.

• Good Website Traffic: While not a strict requirement, having a reasonable amount of organic traffic to your platform can improve your chances of approval. It shows that your content is attracting visitors, which is appealing to advertisers.

• Ad Placement Compliance: Your website or content platform should have adequate space and compliance with AdSense's ad placement policies. This includes not placing ads on restricted areas or implementing excessive ads that negatively impact user experience.

• Website/Blog Policies: For websites or blogs, it's beneficial to have essential pages like About Us, Contact, and Privacy Policy. These pages add credibility and transparency to your platform.

• Supported Languages and Countries: AdSense supports multiple languages and countries. Ensure your content and primary audience align with the supported languages and regions.

• No Previous AdSense Account Issues: If you've had a previous AdSense account, ensure it's in good standing. Past issues like policy violations, suspensions, or terminations can affect your eligibility for a new account.

Remember that meeting these criteria doesn't guarantee automatic approval for an AdSense account. Google reviews each application individually and may take factors like content quality, adherence to policies, and the overall user experience into account before approving an account for monetization through AdSense.

ADSENSE POLICIES AND GUIDELINES

AdSense has specific policies and guidelines that content creators and publishers must adhere to in order to use the platform for monetization. These policies are designed to maintain a high standard of content quality, ensure a positive user experience, and comply with legal requirements. Here's a detailed explanation of AdSense policies and guidelines:

1. Content Policies:

• Original Content: AdSense requires original and unique content. Avoid copying or plagiarizing content from other sources.

• Prohibited Content: Certain content is prohibited, including adult content, copyrighted material without proper authorization, violent content, illegal activities, hate speech, and deceptive practices.

• User-generated Content: If your platform includes user-generated content (comments, forums, etc.), monitor and moderate it to ensure it complies with AdSense policies.

2. Ad Placement Policies:

• Ad Density: Avoid placing too many ads on a single page. AdSense has specific guidelines regarding the number of ads allowed per page.

• Ad Behavior: Ads should not mimic content or deceive users into clicking them. They should be clearly distinguishable from the website's content.

• Ad Placement: Ads should not be placed in areas that lead to accidental clicks, such as near navigational elements, pop-ups, or deceptive locations.

3. Website Quality and Navigation:

• Website Quality: Ensure your website offers a good user experience, is easy to navigate, and provides valuable content. It should be free from broken links, excessive pop-ups, or disruptive elements.

• Mobile Optimization: Websites should be mobile-friendly and provide a good experience across different devices.

• Navigation and Transparency: Clearly label navigation elements and ensure users can easily find their way around your site. Include essential pages like About Us, Contact, and Privacy Policy.

4. Policy Enforcement and Compliance:

• Policy Violations: Violations of AdSense policies can result in warnings, temporary ad serving limitations, or account suspension. Google may notify you of policy violations and provide an opportunity to rectify them.

• Appeals Process: If your account is suspended or disabled, AdSense provides an appeals process to request a review of the decision. You can address issues and request reconsideration.

5. Additional Guidelines:

• Copyright Compliance: Respect copyright laws and do not use copyrighted material without proper authorization.

• Traffic Sources: Avoid artificial traffic generation or methods that manipulate user behavior, such as buying traffic or incentivizing clicks.

• Sensitive Categories: If your content falls under sensitive categories like health, finance, or legal issues, provide accurate and reliable information.

AdSense policies are comprehensive and aim to maintain a fair and safe advertising environment for users, advertisers, and publishers. Violating these policies can lead to ad serving limitations or account termination. Therefore, it's crucial for content creators to familiarize themselves with these policies and ensure ongoing compliance to maintain a healthy relationship with AdSense.

THE TYPES OF CONTENT THAT COMPLY WITH ADSENSE POLICIES

AdSense policies aim to ensure that content aligns with certain standards, maintaining a safe and positive environment for users, advertisers, and publishers. Content that complies with AdSense policies typically includes:

• Original and Valuable Content: Content that is original, unique, and provides value to users. It should offer information, entertainment, or solutions that are not easily found elsewhere.

• Quality Articles and Blog Posts: Well-researched, informative, and well-written articles or blog posts that cater to users' interests and provide valuable insights or guidance.

• Video Content: Original and engaging video content, such as tutorials, reviews, entertainment, or educational videos, that adhere to community guidelines and copyright laws.

• Informative and Engaging Websites: Websites that offer genuine and relevant information, whether it's about news, lifestyle, technology, travel, finance, health, or other niches, in a well-structured and engaging manner.

• User-generated Content (with moderation): Platforms hosting user-generated content (like forums, comments, or user submissions) that are actively moderated to ensure they comply with AdSense policies.

• Mobile Apps with Valuable Functions: Mobile apps that provide useful functions, services, or entertainment, following app store guidelines and not engaging in deceptive practices.

• Compliance with Legal and Ethical Standards: Content that adheres to legal requirements, respects intellectual property rights (no unauthorized use of copyrighted material), and avoids promoting illegal activities or hate speech.

• Transparent and Trustworthy Information: Informational content that is transparent, accurate, and trustworthy, particularly if it relates to sensitive topics like health, finance, legal matters, etc.

• Engaging Multimedia Content: Interactive and engaging multimedia content, such as quizzes, polls, infographics, or interactive elements, that enriches user experience without misleading or deceptive practices.

• Compliance with Google Webmaster Guidelines: Websites that follow Google's Webmaster Guidelines for proper indexing, user experience, and site performance.

It's important to note that compliance with AdSense policies is a continuous responsibility for content creators. Regularly reviewing and updating content to ensure it meets these criteria is crucial to maintain a healthy relationship with AdSense and avoid policy violations or account issues. Adherence to these policies helps in sustaining a positive environment for users and advertisers while ensuring a fair and rewarding experience for content creators.

COMPLIANT AND NON-COMPLIANT CONTENT

Here are examples of compliant and non-compliant content according to AdSense policies:

Compliant Content:

Compliant Article/Blog Post:

• Compliant: An original blog post offering valuable tips on home gardening, providing in-depth insights and practical advice for beginners.

• Non-Compliant: Copy-pasted or spun content from other websites lacking originality or depth.

Compliant Video Content:

• Compliant: A YouTube video tutorial demonstrating DIY home improvement projects, showcasing original ideas and clear instructions.

- Non-Compliant: Videos containing copyrighted music or footage without proper authorization or providing misleading information.

Compliant Website/Platform:

- Compliant: A travel website featuring well-written articles, genuine travel experiences, and high-quality images that offer helpful insights to travelers.

- Non-Compliant: A website hosting illegal download links, adult content, or promoting deceptive schemes.

User-Generated Content (Compliant with Moderation):

- Compliant: A forum discussing photography techniques, actively moderated to remove offensive comments or spam.

- Non-Compliant: A forum filled with hate speech, inappropriate content, or unmoderated comments promoting illegal activities.

Mobile App (Compliant with App Store Guidelines):

- Compliant: A productivity app offering useful tools, adhering to app store guidelines, and providing a clear privacy policy.

- Non-Compliant: An app engaging in deceptive practices, containing misleading advertisements, or requesting unnecessary user data without consent.

Transparent and Trustworthy Information:

• Compliant: A financial blog providing accurate investment advice, transparently disclosing potential risks associated with various investment strategies.

• Non-Compliant: A financial website promoting get-rich-quick schemes or misleading financial advice.

Non-Compliant Content:

• Copyright Infringement: Republished content without authorization, such as articles copied from other websites or using copyrighted images without permission.

• Deceptive Practices: Websites or ads that deceive users with misleading information, false promises, or deceptive marketing tactics.

• Prohibited Content: Content promoting illegal activities, adult content, violence, hate speech, or content that violates privacy or personal information.

• Low-Quality or Thin Content: Websites or blogs with shallow or thin content, lacking substance, and providing little to no value to users.

• Auto-Generated or Scam Content: Automatically generated content, such as spun articles or content created solely to manipulate search engine rankings or deceive users.

• Misleading or Sensationalized Information: Articles or videos containing exaggerated or false claims, sensationalized headlines, or misleading information to attract clicks.

Understanding these examples helps content creators differentiate between compliant and non-compliant content, ensuring they create valuable, original, and trustworthy content that aligns with AdSense policies.

WHAT COULD LEAD TO POLICY VIOLATIONS AND ACCOUNT SUSPENSION

Policy violations and account suspension on AdSense can occur due to various reasons. Understanding these reasons is crucial to avoid violations and maintain a healthy AdSense account. Here are some common factors that could lead to policy violations and account suspension:

1. Prohibited Content:

• Adult Content: Displaying or promoting explicit or adult content, including nudity or sexual content.

• Copyright Violations: Using copyrighted material without proper authorization or permission.

• Illegal Activities: Promoting illegal activities such as hacking, illegal downloads, drugs, or counterfeit goods.

• Hate Speech: Content that promotes discrimination, hate speech, violence, or intolerance towards individuals or groups based on race, religion, ethnicity, etc.

• Deceptive Practices: Engaging in misleading or deceptive practices to manipulate users.

2. Invalid Clicks or Traffic Manipulation:

• Click Fraud: Generating invalid clicks on ads, encouraging clicks from users artificially, or engaging in click exchange programs.

• Traffic Manipulation: Using bots, paid traffic services, or incentivizing users to generate artificial traffic.

3. Ad Placement Issues:

• Ad Placement Violations: Placing ads in restricted areas (e.g., near navigational elements), using deceptive tactics to encourage accidental clicks, or using excessive ads on a single page.

• Inappropriate Ad Behavior: Ads that mimic site content, deceive users, or interfere with site navigation.

4. Low-Quality Content:

• Thin or Shallow Content: Websites or platforms with low-quality, thin, or unoriginal content that doesn't provide value to users.

• Auto-generated Content: Using tools to generate content automatically without adding substantial value.

5. Privacy and User Data Issues:

• Privacy Violations: Collecting and using user data in ways that violate privacy policies or without user consent.

6. Policy Enforcement and Repeated Violations:

• Repeated Violations: Ignoring warnings or repeated policy violations after previous enforcement actions by AdSense.

• Appeals Not Addressed: Failing to address or rectify issues highlighted in policy violation notices or suspension warnings.

7. Non-Compliance with Guidelines:

• Non-Compliance with AdSense Policies: Failing to comply with AdSense program policies, including content, ad placement, and user experience guidelines.

8. Third-Party Ad Behavior:

• Third-Party Ad Networks: Using other ad networks that conflict with AdSense policies or deploying ads from unauthorized sources.

9. Invalid Site Practices:

• Malware or Phishing: Hosting malware, phishing, or malicious software on the website or platform.

10. Legal Compliance Issues:

• Legal Compliance: Violating local or international laws, including those related to gambling, sensitive content, or financial services.

AdSense continuously monitors content and user interactions to ensure compliance with policies. Violations can lead to warnings, temporary ad serving limitations, or account suspension. In severe cases or repeated violations, Google might disable an account permanently.

To avoid policy violations and account issues, content creators should regularly review AdSense policies, create original and high-quality content, maintain transparency, provide a good user experience, and address any compliance issues promptly if notified by Google.

CHAPTER TWO

VARIOUS AD SIZES AND PLACEMENTS

Ad sizes and placements are crucial aspects of an AdSense strategy, influencing Ad performance and user engagement. Here's an explanation of various ad sizes and placements commonly used in AdSense:

Ad Sizes:

Leaderboard (728x90):

• Horizontal ad placed at the top or bottom of a webpage.

• Suitable for headers or footers and generally used for desktop viewing.

Banner (468x60 or 320x50):

• Smaller horizontal Ads that can fit within content or at the top/bottom of mobile screens.

• Often used within blog posts or below the navigation bar.

Skyscraper (120x600 or 160x600):

• Vertical ad units placed in the sidebar of a webpage.

• Typically used in the sidebar for better visibility and interaction.

Rectangle (300x250 or 336x280):

• Medium rectangle Ad size that fits well within content or sidebars.

• Versatile size suitable for embedding in articles, below images, or within text.

Half Page (300x600):

• Larger vertical Ad unit suitable for sidebars or embedded within content.

• Provides a larger canvas for advertisers to showcase content.

Large Rectangle (336x280):

• Larger square or rectangular ad, suitable for content-rich websites.

• Often placed within articles, between paragraphs, or as standalone units within content.

Responsive Ads:

• Ads that automatically adjust their size and format based on the device and available ad space.

• AdSense offers responsive ad units that adapt to different screen sizes for optimal viewing.

Ad Placements:

Above the Fold:

• Ads placed within the visible area of a webpage without scrolling.

• Ensures high visibility and engagement, often placed at the top of the page.

Below the Fold:

• Ads positioned below the visible area, requiring users to scroll to view.

• Typically used for additional ad units or to avoid excessive top-of-page clutter.

In-Content:

• Ads embedded within the content of articles or posts.

• Blends naturally with the content for higher engagement.

Sidebar or Widget Area:

• Ads placed in the sidebar or widget areas of websites or blogs.

• Skyscraper or rectangle ads are commonly used in this space.

Header or Footer:

• Ads placed at the top (header) or bottom (footer) of a webpage.

• Often used for leaderboard or banner ad sizes.

Interstitial Ads:

• Full-screen ads that appear between content pages or during navigation.

• Commonly used in apps or mobile websites for engaging users.

Native Ads:

• Ads that match the design and style of the website or content.

• Blends seamlessly with the content for a non-disruptive user experience.

Choosing the right ad size and placement depends on factors like website layout, user behavior, and content type. Experimentation with different sizes and placements, along with adherence to AdSense policies on ad placement, can help optimize ad performance and maximize revenue while maintaining a positive user experience.

Optimizing display ad performance is crucial for maximizing revenue and enhancing user experience. Here are some tips to optimize the performance of display ads in AdSense:

1. Ad Placement Optimization:

• Above the Fold Placement: Place ads within the visible area without scrolling for better visibility and higher click-through rates.

• In-Content Ads: Embed ads within the content to blend naturally with the material, increasing user interaction without disrupting the experience.

• Experiment with Different Positions: Test various ad positions (header, sidebar, footer, etc.) to find the most effective placements for your audience and content.

2. Use a Variety of Ad Sizes:

• Responsive Ads: Utilize responsive ad units that adapt to different screen sizes and devices, ensuring optimal viewing and engagement.

• Test Multiple Sizes: Experiment with various ad sizes to understand which ones perform best on your website or platform. Common sizes include rectangles, banners, and skyscrapers.

3. Optimize Ad Design and Visuals:

• Attractive Ad Design: Create visually appealing ads that are relevant to your content and audience. Use high-quality images, compelling copy, and clear calls-to-action.

• Blend Ads with Website Design: Customize ad styles to match the look and feel of your website or platform. Native-style ads often perform better by appearing more integrated and less intrusive.

4. Improve Website User Experience:

• Page Load Speed: Ensure your website loads quickly to prevent user frustration and improve ad viewability. Slow loading times can lead to lower ad impressions.

• Mobile Optimization: Prioritize mobile optimization as mobile traffic continues to grow. Make sure ads display properly on mobile devices for a seamless user experience.

5. Monitor and Analyze Performance:

• Use AdSense Analytics: Monitor ad performance using AdSense analytics. Analyze metrics such as click-through rates (CTR), viewability, earnings per click (EPC), and ad fill rates.

• A/B Testing: Conduct A/B tests to compare different ad placements, sizes, and designs. Test one variable at a time to understand what works best for your audience.

6. AdSense Policy Compliance:

• Ad Placement Policy: Adhere to AdSense ad placement policies to avoid violations. Improper ad placement might lead to penalties or lower ad serving.

• Content Relevance: Ensure ad relevance to your content. Irrelevant ads may reduce user engagement and click-through rates.

7. Consider Ad Blocking and Ad Quality:

• Ad Blockers: Be aware of ad blockers and their impact on ad impressions. Offer value to users to encourage them to disable ad blockers on your site.

• Ad Quality: Monitor the quality of ads displayed. Report any low-quality or irrelevant ads to maintain a positive user experience.

By implementing these strategies, content creators can optimize display ad performance, increase user engagement, and maximize revenue potential through AdSense. Regular monitoring, testing, and adaptation based on insights will help in achieving better ad performance over time.

HOW TO INTEGRATE AND OPTIMIZE VIDEO ADS WITHIN CONTENT

Integrating and optimizing video ads within content can significantly enhance user engagement and revenue generation. Here's a step-by-step guide to effectively integrate and optimize video ads:

1. Understand Video Ad Formats:

• In-stream Video Ads: These ads play before, during, or after video content. They can be skippable or non-skippable.

• Out-stream Video Ads: Standalone video ads that appear within non-video content, like articles or feeds.

2. Integrate Video Ad Units:

• Select Suitable Video Ad Units: Choose appropriate video ad units from AdSense (such as in-stream or out-stream) based on your content and user preferences.

• Implement Video Player Integration: Integrate a video player compatible with AdSense. Popular video players include JW Player, Video.js, or Google's IMA SDK for advanced integration.

3. Optimize Video Ad Placement:

• Strategic Placement: Embed video ads at natural breakpoints in your video content, such as before a video starts or during transitions for in-stream ads.

• Out-stream Ad Placement: Place out-stream video ads within your content where users are likely to engage, like within articles or between sections.

4. Create Engaging Video Content:

• High-Quality Video Production: Produce high-quality, engaging video content that aligns with your audience's interests and provides value.

• Attention-Grabbing Beginnings: For in-stream ads, capture viewers' attention quickly to reduce the likelihood of skipping the ad.

5. Use AdSense Video Ad Settings:

• Ad Customization: Customize ad settings in AdSense, such as ad formats, skippable or non-skippable ads, and frequency capping, to suit your audience preferences.

• Targeting Options: Utilize targeting options provided by AdSense to reach specific demographics or interests within your audience.

6. Monitor and Optimize:

• Track Performance Metrics: Monitor video ad performance metrics such as view rates, completion rates, click-through rates, and earnings using AdSense analytics.

• A/B Testing: Experiment with different Ad placements, lengths, or formats using A/B testing to understand what resonates best with your audience.

7. Ensure User Experience:

• Balanced Ad Frequency: Avoid excessive ad interruptions to maintain a positive user experience. Balance Ad frequency to prevent user annoyance.

• Responsive Design: Ensure video Ad units are responsive and adapt well to different screen sizes and devices for seamless user experience.

8. Compliance and Policy Adherence:

• AdSense Policies: Adhere to AdSense policies regarding video ad content, placement, and user experience to prevent violations and ensure continued monetization.

• Ad Quality: Ensure video ads align with your content and maintain high-quality standards. Report any low-quality or irrelevant ads to AdSense.

By integrating video ads effectively within your content and optimizing their placement, content creators can provide engaging user experiences while maximizing revenue opportunities through AdSense video ads. Regular monitoring, experimentation, and adherence to policies are essential for sustained success in video ad optimization.

BEST PRACTICES FOR VIDEO AD MONETIZATION

Video ad monetization can be optimized by following these best practices:

1. Diversify Ad Formats:

• In-Stream Ads: Utilize pre-roll, mid-roll, or post-roll video ads that play before, during, or after video content.

• Out-Stream Ads: Incorporate standalone video ads within non-video content, like articles or feeds.

2. Select Relevant Ad Units:

• Choose Ad Units Wisely: Select appropriate ad units based on your content and audience preferences.

• Experiment with Formats: Test various ad formats (skippable vs. non-skippable) to determine what resonates best with your audience.

3. Implement Effective Ad Placement:

• Strategic Placement: Embed ads at natural breakpoints in your video content, ensuring they complement rather than disrupt the viewing experience.

• Frequency Capping: Avoid overwhelming viewers by limiting the frequency of Ad displays within a specific time frame.

4. Create Engaging Video Content:

• High-Quality Production: Produce compelling, high-quality video content that captivates viewers and aligns with their interests.

• Optimize Length: Balance content and ad length to maintain engagement without deterring viewers with excessively long ads.

5. Utilize Targeting and Personalization:

• Audience Segmentation: Use AdSense targeting options to reach specific demographics or interests within your audience.

• Personalized Ads: Employ personalized Ad targeting based on user behavior or preferences for higher engagement.

6. Optimize Monetization Settings:

• Ad Settings Customization: Tailor ad settings in AdSense to suit your audience's preferences, such as ad formats, skippable options, or frequency.

• Ad Load Optimization: Experiment with the number and placement of ads to strike a balance between revenue and user experience.

7. Track Performance Metrics:

• Analytics Monitoring: Regularly monitor video ad performance metrics (e.g., view rates, completion rates, CTRs) using AdSense analytics.

• A/B Testing: Conduct A/B tests to compare different ad placements, lengths, or formats to identify what works best for your audience.

8. Ensure Responsive Design:

• Cross-Device Compatibility: Ensure video ad units are responsive and display seamlessly across different screen sizes and devices.

• Optimized Mobile Experience: Prioritize mobile optimization as mobile traffic continues to increase.

9. Adherence to Policies:

• AdSense Policy Compliance: Adhere to AdSense policies regarding video ad content, placement, and user experience to avoid violations and maintain monetization eligibility.

• Ad Quality Control: Ensure video ads maintain high-quality standards and are relevant to your content. Report any inappropriate or irrelevant ads.

By implementing these best practices, content creators can optimize video ad monetization, maximize revenue potential, and provide a positive user experience while leveraging AdSense's video ad features. Regular monitoring, experimentation, and policy compliance are key to sustained success in video Ad monetization.

NATIVE ADVERTISING

Native advertising is a form of paid advertising that matches the form, function, and style of the platform on which it appears. The primary goal of native advertising is to seamlessly blend in with the surrounding content, providing a non-disruptive and cohesive user experience while delivering promotional messaging.

Key characteristics of native advertising include:

• Seamless Integration: Native ads are designed to look and feel like the surrounding non-advertising content, matching the visual and contextual design of the platform.

• Contextual Relevance: These ads aim to be contextually relevant to the platform and the user's interests, offering content that aligns with the audience's expectations.

• Engagement-Focused: Rather than interrupting the user experience, native ads aim to engage and attract users by delivering valuable or interesting content.

• Various Formats: Native ads can take on different formats, such as articles, videos, sponsored posts, promoted listings, or in-feed ads, depending on the platform.

• Disclosure of Sponsorship: While native ads blend with the platform's content, they should be clearly labeled or disclosed as sponsored content to ensure transparency.

Examples of native advertising include sponsored articles on news websites, promoted social media posts, recommended content on publishing platforms, and product placements in online videos. Native advertising is valued for its ability to generate higher user engagement, as it often doesn't disrupt the user's experience while still delivering advertising messages effectively.

INTEGRATION METHODS OF NATIVE ADVERTISING

Native advertising integrates into various platforms through different methods to seamlessly blend with the surrounding content. Here are common integration methods used in native advertising:

1. In-Feed Ads:

• Social Media Feeds: Sponsored posts or content that appears within the regular feed on social media platforms like Facebook, Twitter, or Instagram.

• Website Content Feeds: Native ads integrated into the content feed of websites, such as news articles, blogs, or forums, matching the look and feel of the surrounding posts or articles.

2. Paid Search Units:

• Search Engine Ads: Paid search ads that appear in search engine results, resembling organic search listings but marked as "sponsored" or "ad."

3. Promoted Listings:

• E-commerce Platforms: Sponsored product listings or recommendations that blend with the organic listings on e-commerce sites like Amazon, eBay, or Etsy.

4. Branded Content:

• Sponsored Articles or Stories: Articles, blog posts, or stories created by brands or advertisers and published on websites, seamlessly integrating with the site's editorial content.

5. Sponsored Video Content:

• Video Platforms: Sponsored videos on platforms like YouTube or streaming services, which resemble regular content but are marked as sponsored or promoted.

6. Native Display Ads:

• Custom Display Ad Units: Display ads designed to match the visual style and context of the website or app where they're placed, appearing as part of the content.

7. Custom Integration:

• Custom Solutions: Unique and tailored ad integrations that fit the specific format and design of a particular platform or publisher, often requiring collaboration between advertisers and publishers.

8. Influencer Marketing:

• Influencer Collaboration: Sponsored content created by influencers in partnership with brands, where the content aligns with the influencer's style and audience interests.

9. Content Recommendation Widgets:

• Content Discovery Platforms: Recommendations of sponsored content within content recommendation widgets on websites, offering users additional articles or content.

10. Contextual Integration:

• Contextual Relevance: Ads presented in a contextually relevant manner based on user behavior, interests, or content consumption patterns.

These methods aim to create a cohesive user experience by seamlessly integrating promotional content with the platform's regular content. Native advertising, when executed effectively, enhances user engagement and brand visibility by delivering relevant, non-disruptive content within the user's natural browsing or consumption flow.

TIPS FOR BLENDING NATIVE ADS SEAMLESSLY INTO CONTENT

Blending native ads seamlessly into content involves careful planning and execution to ensure they fit naturally within the user experience. Here are tips for effectively blending native ads into content:

1. Match Visual Design:

• Design Consistency: Ensure the ad's visual elements, such as colors, fonts, and style, match those of the surrounding content to create a cohesive look.

• Customized Ad Formats: Tailor ad formats to resemble the design elements of the platform where they're displayed, ensuring they blend seamlessly.

2. Contextual Relevance:

• Relevant Content: Create ad content that aligns with the interests of the platform's audience and the surrounding content to maintain relevance.

• Targeted Messaging: Tailor the ad message to fit the context without appearing overly promotional, offering value or information that complements the user's browsing experience.

3. Disclosure and Transparency:

• Clear Disclosure: Clearly label the native ad as "sponsored," "promoted," or "ad" to maintain transparency and avoid misleading users.

• Non-Intrusive Disclosure: Incorporate disclosure seamlessly without disrupting the flow of content or user experience.

4. Engaging and Valuable Content:

• Quality Content: Offer high-quality and engaging content that educates, entertains, or informs the audience, encouraging interaction and sharing.

• Storytelling Approach: Use storytelling or narrative techniques to engage users, making the ad content feel more like a natural part of the platform.

5. Native Ad Placement:

• Strategic Placement: Position the native ad where users are accustomed to seeing similar content, ensuring it fits naturally within the content flow.

• In-Context Integration: Embed the ad within relevant content sections to make it feel integrated rather than disruptive.

6. Test and Refine:

• A/B Testing: Experiment with different ad placements, designs, or messaging to identify what resonates best with the audience without compromising the user experience.

• Performance Monitoring: Continuously monitor ad performance metrics to refine and optimize native ad strategies based on user engagement and conversion data.

7. Respect User Experience:

• Non-Disruptive Approach: Avoid overly aggressive or intrusive ad placements that might disrupt the user's browsing or reading experience.

• Value-Oriented Approach: Ensure the ad adds value to users by providing useful information, solving a problem, or offering relevant products or services.

8. Collaborate with Publishers:

• Partnership with Publishers: Work closely with publishers to create native ads that align with their content style and audience preferences.

• Publisher Guidelines: Adhere to publisher guidelines and recommendations to ensure seamless integration without compromising the platform's integrity.

By following these tips, advertisers and content creators can create native ads that seamlessly integrate with the content, providing value to users while maintaining the authenticity and integrity of the platform.

CHAPTER THREE

THE DIFFERENT AD FORMAT

Ad formats vary across different platforms and advertising mediums. Here's an overview of various ad formats used in digital advertising:

1. Display Ads:

• Banner Ads: Rectangular graphical ads placed on web pages, available in various sizes (e.g., leaderboard - 728x90, medium rectangle - 300x250).

• Interstitial Ads: Full-screen ads that appear between content pages or during navigation on mobile apps or websites.

• Expandable Ads: Ads that expand beyond their initial size upon user interaction, providing more information or content.

2. Search Engine Ads:

• Text Ads: Text-based ads displayed alongside search engine results based on keywords or user queries (e.g., Google Ads, Bing Ads).

• Shopping Ads: Product-based ads displaying images, prices, and details for specific products relevant to the search query.

3. Video Ads:

• In-Stream Video Ads: Video ads that play before, during, or after video content on platforms like YouTube or streaming services. They can be skippable or non-skippable.

• Out-Stream Video Ads: Standalone video ads that appear within non-video content, like articles or feeds, usually auto-playing when in view.

4. Native Ads:

• In-Feed Ads: Ads seamlessly integrated within content feeds, such as social media feeds or website content feeds, matching the platform's style and format.

• Sponsored Content: Promotional content designed to match the style and context of the platform where it's published, such as sponsored articles or sponsored posts.

5. Social Media Ads:

• Sponsored Posts: Paid posts on social media platforms that resemble organic content but are promoted to a specific audience based on targeting.

• Carousel Ads: Ads featuring multiple images or videos that users can swipe through, engaging with a series of content within a single ad.

6. Rich Media Ads:

• Interactive Ads: Ads with interactive elements like games, quizzes, or videos that encourage user engagement beyond a static display.

• Dynamic Ads: Customizable ads that change content based on user data, displaying personalized information or products.

7. Mobile Ads:

• Mobile Banner Ads: Smaller banner ads specifically designed for mobile devices, often placed at the top or bottom of mobile websites or apps.

• App Install Ads: Ads encouraging users to download or install mobile applications directly from app stores.

8. Audio Ads:

• Streaming Audio Ads: Audio-based ads played during audio content streaming, like podcasts or music streaming services.

• Voice Ads: Ads optimized for voice-enabled devices and virtual assistants, providing spoken content or interaction.

Each ad format has its unique characteristics, purposes, and targeting options. Advertisers often choose specific formats based on campaign goals, target audience, and the platform where they plan to display the ads, aiming to maximize engagement and achieve desired outcomes.

STEP-BY-STEP GUIDE TO CREATE DISPLAY ADS

Creating display ads through Google AdSense involves several steps to ensure effective implementation. Here's a step-by-step guide:

Step 1: Access Your AdSense Account

• Sign in to AdSense: Visit the AdSense website and log in to your account using your credentials.

Step 2: Create a New Ad Unit

• Navigate to "Ads" Section: Inside your AdSense account, find and click on the "Ads" tab or section.

• Click on "+New ad unit": Select the option to create a new ad unit.

• Choose Ad Type and Format: Specify the ad type (Display ads) and select the ad size and format you prefer. Consider responsive ad units for better adaptability across devices.

• Configure Ad Settings: Set up additional preferences, such as ad style (colors, fonts), backup ads (optional), and ad type (text, image, or rich media).

Step 3: Customize Ad Appearance (Optional)

• Customize Ad Style: Adjust colors, fonts, and other visual aspects to match the look and feel of your website or platform. Ensure it's visually appealing and blends well with your content.

• Preview Your Ad: Use the preview function to see how the Ad will appear on different devices and screen sizes.

Step 4: Get Ad Code

• Generate Ad Code: Once satisfied with the settings, click on the "Save and get code" or similar option to generate the ad code snippet.

Step 5: Implement Ad Code on Your Website

• Copy the Ad Code: Copy the provided ad code snippet.

• Paste the Code into Your Website: Access the HTML of your website or content management system. Paste the ad code into the relevant sections of your webpage where you want the ad to appear.

• Save Changes and Publish: Save the changes to your website and publish the updated content.

Step 6: Monitor and Optimize

• Monitor Ad Performance: Regularly check your AdSense account to track the performance of your display ads. Analyze metrics like CTR (Click-Through Rate), RPM (Revenue per Mille), and ad viewability.

• Optimize for Better Results: Use the insights gathered from performance metrics to make data-driven optimizations. Experiment with different ad placements, formats, and styles to improve ad performance.

Step 7: Adhere to Policies

• Comply with AdSense Policies: Ensure your display ads comply with AdSense policies and guidelines to prevent potential issues or account violations.

By following these steps, you can create and implement display ads through Google AdSense effectively. Regularly monitoring performance and making necessary optimizations are key to maximizing the effectiveness of your display Ad campaigns.

STEP-BY-STEP GUIDE TO CREATE VIDEO ADS

Creating video ads through Google AdSense involves a process that integrates with Google Ads (formerly known as Google AdWords) for video campaigns. Here's a step-by-step guide:

Step 1: Access Your Google Ads Account

• Sign in to Google Ads: Go to the Google Ads website (ads.google.com) and log in using your Google account credentials.

Step 2: Create a New Video Campaign

• Click on "+Campaign": In your Google Ads account, click the blue "+" button to create a new campaign.

• Select Campaign Type: Choose "New campaign" and then select the campaign goal that aligns with your advertising objectives. For video ads, choose options like "Brand Awareness and Reach" or "Product and Brand Consideration."

• Choose Campaign Subtype: Select the campaign subtype that includes video ads, such as "Video."

Step 3: Set Campaign Details

• Enter Campaign Settings: Set up the campaign details, including campaign name, bidding strategy, budget, start and end dates, target audience, and Ad delivery method.

• Choose Ad Group Type: Create an ad group within your campaign to organize your ads and set targeting options for specific audiences or demographics.

Step 4: Create a Video Ad

• Select Video Ad Format: Choose the type of video ad format you want to create, such as TrueView in-stream ads, TrueView video discovery ads, or bumper ads.

• Upload Video or Create Ad: Upload the video ad content or use YouTube links if the video is hosted on YouTube. Ensure the video follows Google's ad specifications regarding length, format, and content.

• Set Ad Settings: Configure ad settings, including ad name, call-to-action (CTA), headline, description, and display URL.

Step 5: Customize Ad Appearance (Optional)

• Customize Video Ad Elements: Adjust ad elements such as text overlays, end screens, or companion banners to enhance engagement and visibility.

Step 6: Choose Targeting and Placement

• Set Targeting Options: Define the target audience by selecting demographics, interests, keywords, placements, or remarketing lists to reach specific users.

• Choose Ad Placement: Select where your video ads will appear, such as YouTube videos, websites, apps, or within the Google Display Network.

Step 7: Review and Launch Campaign

• Review Campaign Details: Double-check all settings, targeting options, and ad content to ensure accuracy and alignment with your advertising goals.

• Launch Campaign: Once everything is reviewed and set, launch your video ad campaign to begin running your ads.

Step 8: Monitor and Optimize

• Monitor Ad Performance: Regularly review performance metrics like views, view rates, click-through rates, and conversions within your Google Ads account.

• Optimize for Better Results: Use the insights from performance data to make adjustments and optimizations to improve the effectiveness of your video ad campaigns.

By following these steps within your Google Ads account, you can create and run video Ad campaigns effectively, reaching your target audience and maximizing the impact of your video ads.

STEP-BY-STEP GUIDE TO CREATE SEARCH ENGINE ADS

Creating search engine ads, commonly done through Google Ads, involves a process to craft text-based ads that appear on search engine results pages (SERPs). Here's a step-by-step guide:

Step 1: Access Your Google Ads Account

• Sign in to Google Ads: Go to the Google Ads website (ads.google.com) and log in using your Google account credentials.

Step 2: Create a New Campaign

• Click on "+Campaign": In your Google Ads account, click the blue "+" button to create a new campaign.

• Select Campaign Type: Choose the campaign goal that aligns with your objectives, such as "Sales," "Leads," or "Website Traffic."

• Choose Campaign Subtype: Select "Search" as the campaign subtype for creating text-based search ads.

Step 3: Set Campaign Details

• Enter Campaign Settings: Set up campaign details, including campaign name, bidding strategy, budget, start and end dates, target locations, and languages.

• Choose Network and Devices: Select the networks where you want your ads to appear, such as Google Search Network, Search Partners, and specific device types (desktop, mobile, tablet).

Step 4: Create Ad Groups

• Create Ad Groups: Organize your ads by creating ad groups within the campaign. Each ad group can have specific keywords and ads targeting different audiences or themes.

Step 5: Craft Text Ads

• Write Ad Copy: Create text-based ads with compelling headlines, descriptions, and relevant keywords. Follow character limits for headlines and descriptions provided by Google.

• Add Ad Extensions: Enhance your ads by adding extensions such as Sitelink Extensions, Callout Extensions, or Location Extensions to provide additional information and improve ad visibility.

Step 6: Choose Keywords and Targeting

• Select Keywords: Choose relevant keywords for each ad group that match user search queries. Use Google's Keyword Planner to find relevant keywords with appropriate search volumes.

• Set Keyword Match Types: Specify keyword match types (broad match, phrase match, exact match, or broad match modifier) to control how your ads are triggered.

Step 7: Set Bids and Budget

• Determine Bidding Strategy: Choose a bidding strategy based on your campaign objectives, such as manual CPC (Cost-Per-Click) or automated bidding strategies like Target CPA or Target ROAS.

• Set Bid Amounts: Define maximum CPC bids for keywords and adjust bids based on keyword performance and competition.

Step 8: Review and Launch Campaign

• Review Ad Preview: Preview and review your ad content and settings to ensure accuracy and relevance.

• Set Campaign Live: Once everything is reviewed, launch your search engine ad campaign to start displaying your ads to potential users.

Step 9: Monitor and Optimize

• Monitor Ad Performance: Regularly monitor key metrics such as CTR, conversion rates, quality score, and ad positions within your Google Ads account.

• Optimize Ad Campaign: Use performance insights to make adjustments, refine ad copy, add negative keywords, and optimize bidding for better results.

Following these steps within Google Ads enables you to create effective search engine ads that target relevant audiences, increase visibility, and drive traffic to your website or landing pages. Regular monitoring and optimization are crucial for maximizing the effectiveness of your search ads.

Creating social media ads involves using the advertising platforms provided by various social media channels such as Facebook, Instagram, Twitter, LinkedIn, and others. Here's a general step-by-step guide that applies to most social media platforms:

Step 1: Choose the Social Media Platform

• Select the Platform: Determine which social media platform aligns best with your target audience and advertising goals. Common choices include Facebook, Instagram, Twitter, LinkedIn, Pinterest, etc.

Step 2: Access the Ad Management Platform

• Log in to the Ad Manager: Access the advertising management section provided by the chosen social media platform. It's often named "Ads Manager" or "Business Manager."

Step 3: Create a New Ad Campaign

• Click on "+Create" or "Create Campaign": Start a new ad campaign within the Ad Manager.

• Select Campaign Objective: Choose the objective that matches your marketing goals, such as brand awareness, website traffic, conversions, lead generation, etc.

Step 4: Define Your Target Audience

• Set Targeting Options: Define your audience based on demographics, interests, behaviors, locations, or other relevant criteria. Narrow down your audience to reach the most relevant users.

Step 5: Choose Ad Placement and Format

• Select Ad Placement: Choose where your ads will appear on the platform, including news feeds, stories, sidebar, or specific placements within the platform.

• Choose Ad Format: Select the ad format suitable for your campaign, such as image ads, video ads, carousel ads, slideshow ads, or text-based ads.

Step 6: Create Ad Content

• Design Ad Creative: Create engaging and visually appealing ad content that aligns with the chosen format. This may include images, videos, ad copy, headlines, and call-to-action buttons.

• Add Relevant Text and Links: Include compelling ad text, relevant links (e.g., to your website or landing page), and a clear call-to-action to encourage user interaction.

Step 7: Set Budget and Schedule

• Determine Budget: Set your daily or lifetime budget for the ad campaign. Define the amount you're willing to spend based on your advertising goals.

• Schedule Ad Run Time: Specify the start and end dates for your ad campaign or run it continuously based on your objectives.

Step 8: Review and Launch

• Preview and Review: Double-check all elements of your ad campaign, including targeting, ad content, budget, and schedule, to ensure accuracy and effectiveness.

• Launch the Ad Campaign: Once reviewed and finalized, launch your social media ad campaign to start delivering your ads to the selected audience.

Step 9: Monitor and Optimize

• Monitor Ad Performance: Regularly track key performance metrics provided by the platform, such as impressions, clicks, CTR, conversions, and ROI.

• Optimize Ad Campaign: Use insights gained from performance data to make adjustments, refine targeting, tweak ad content, and optimize budget allocation for better results.

Following these steps will help you create and launch social media ads effectively, allowing you to reach your target audience, increase brand visibility, and achieve your marketing objectives on various social media platforms.

STEP-BY-STEP GUIDE TO CREATE NATIVE ADS

Creating native ads involves crafting ads that seamlessly blend with the form and function of the platform they appear on, offering a non-disruptive advertising experience. Here's a step-by-step guide to creating native ads:

Step 1: Select the Native Advertising Platform

• Choose a Platform: Identify platforms that support native advertising, such as social media channels (Facebook, Instagram), content discovery platforms (Taboola, Outbrain), or publisher websites.

Step 2: Access the Native Advertising Platform

• Access Ad Creation Tools: Log in to the advertising dashboard or ad creation section provided by the chosen native advertising platform.

Step 3: Create a New Ad Campaign

• Initiate New Campaign: Click on the option to create a new ad campaign within the platform.

• Choose Campaign Objective: Select the campaign objective aligning with your marketing goals, such as brand awareness, traffic, conversions, or app installs.

Step 4: Define Your Target Audience

• Set Audience Targeting: Define the target audience based on demographics, interests, behaviors, or specific criteria provided by the platform.

Step 5: Choose Native Ad Format

• Select Native Ad Format: Choose the native ad format suitable for the platform, which might include in-feed ads, recommended content widgets, sponsored content, or promoted listings.

• Customize Ad Placement: Specify where you want your native ads to appear within the platform, ensuring they blend seamlessly with the user experience.

Step 6: Create Ad Content

• Craft Engaging Ad Content: Develop compelling ad content that matches the native format, such as engaging headlines, descriptive text, high-quality images, or videos.

• Match Ad Style to Platform: Ensure the ad's design, tone, and style align with the platform's natural content to appear native and non-intrusive.

Step 7: Set Budget and Schedule

• Determine Ad Budget: Set a daily or overall budget for the native ad campaign based on your advertising goals and spending capacity.

• Schedule Ad Run Time: Define the start and end dates for your native ad campaign or let it run continuously as per your marketing objectives.

Step 8: Review and Launch

• Review Ad Preview: Preview and review your native ad content and settings to ensure it's in line with your campaign objectives and adheres to platform guidelines.

• Launch the Ad Campaign: Once everything is reviewed and finalized, launch your native ad campaign to start displaying your ads to the target audience.

Step 9: Monitor and Optimize

• Monitor Ad Performance: Regularly track key performance metrics provided by the platform, such as impressions, engagement, click-through rates, conversions, and ROI.

• Optimize Ad Campaign: Use performance insights to make adjustments, refine targeting, tweak ad content, and optimize budget allocation for better results.

By following these steps, you can effectively create native ads that seamlessly integrate with the chosen platform, ensuring a non-disruptive and engaging advertising experience for your audience.

STEP-BY-STEP GUIDE TO CREATE RICH MEDIA ADS

Creating rich media ads involves crafting interactive and engaging ad formats that go beyond static images or text-based ads. Here's a step-by-step guide to creating rich media ads:

Step 1: Access the Ad Platform or Ad Creation Tool

• Log In to Ad Creation Interface: Access the advertising platform or ad creation tool that supports rich media ad formats. This could be Google Ads, a specific ad network, or a creative platform like Adobe Animate or Google Web Designer.

Step 2: Start a New Ad Campaign

• Create a New Campaign: Initiate a new ad campaign within the platform or tool. Select the appropriate campaign objective based on your marketing goals.

Step 3: Choose Rich Media Ad Format

• Select Rich Media Ad Format: Choose the specific rich media ad format you want to create, such as HTML5 ads, interactive banners, expandable ads, interstitials, video ads, or carousel ads.

• Specify Ad Dimensions: Determine the ad size or dimensions suitable for the Ad format and where it will be displayed (e.g., desktop, mobile, specific placements).

Step 4: Design Interactive Ad Content

• Create Ad Content: Design interactive and visually engaging Ad content using multimedia elements such as images, animations, videos, audio, interactive features, or custom HTML/CSS/JS code.

• Ensure Mobile Responsiveness: Ensure your rich media ad is responsive and functions well across various devices and screen sizes.

Step 5: Incorporate Interactivity

• Add Interactive Elements: Implement interactive features like clickable buttons, expandable sections, rollover effects, quizzes, games, or other engaging functionalities within the ad.

Step 6: Add Tracking and Measurement

• Include Tracking Tags: Integrate tracking tags or pixels to monitor ad performance and track user interactions, such as clicks, interactions, conversions, or video views.

Step 7: Set Budget and Schedule

• Determine Ad Budget: Set a budget for your rich media ad campaign, specifying the maximum amount you're willing to spend.

• Schedule Ad Run Time: Define the start and end dates for the ad campaign or set it to run continuously based on your marketing objectives.

Step 8: Review and Launch

• Preview and Test: Review the ad preview and test its functionality across different browsers and devices to ensure it works as intended.

• Launch the Ad Campaign: Once thoroughly reviewed and finalized, launch your rich media ad campaign to start delivering your interactive ads to the target audience.

Step 9: Monitor and Optimize

• Monitor Ad Performance: Regularly monitor key performance metrics like interactions, engagement rates, click-through rates, conversions, and ROI using the ad platform's reporting tools.

• Optimize Ad Campaign: Use performance data insights to optimize the ad campaign, refine targeting, enhance interactivity, adjust ad content, or reallocate budget for better results.

By following these steps, you can effectively create engaging rich media ads that captivate audiences, encourage interaction, and deliver an immersive advertising experience across various digital platforms.

STEP-BY-STEP GUIDE TO CREATE AUDIO ADS

Creating audio ads involves crafting compelling audio content for advertising on various platforms like radio, streaming services, or podcasts. Here's a step-by-step guide to create audio ads:

Step 1: Define Your Ad's Objective and Target Audience

• Identify Your Goals: Determine the primary objective of your audio ad campaign, such as brand awareness, driving traffic, promoting a product, or generating leads.

• Understand Your Audience: Define your target audience demographics, interests, behaviors, and preferences to tailor the message effectively.

Step 2: Choose the Platform for Ad Placement

• Select the Audio Platform: Decide where you want to place your audio ads, such as radio stations, streaming music services (Spotify, Pandora), podcasts, or other audio channels.

Step 3: Plan the Ad Content

• Script Development: Craft a compelling script for your audio ad. Keep it concise, engaging, and aligned with your brand's tone and messaging.

• Voice Talent and Recording: Choose professional voice talent or record the script with high-quality audio equipment to ensure clarity and impact.

Step 4: Format and Length

• Determine Ad Length: Consider the optimal length for your audio ad based on the platform and audience preferences (common lengths include 15 seconds, 30 seconds, or 60 seconds).

• Format the Ad Content: Organize the script to fit the chosen ad length while effectively delivering the key message and call-to-action (CTA).

Step 5: Add Branding Elements

• Include Branding Elements: Incorporate brand mentions, slogans, or jingles into the ad to reinforce brand recall and association.

Step 6: Review and Finalize

• Review and Refine: Listen to the recorded audio ad, and ensure it aligns with your goals, resonates with the target audience, and effectively communicates the intended message.

Step 7: Distribution and Placement

• Select Ad Placement: Work with the chosen platform or ad network to place your audio ad in the appropriate slots, ensuring it reaches your target audience effectively.

Step 8: Monitor and Measure Performance

• Track Ad Performance: Utilize tracking tools or data provided by the platform to monitor ad performance, including metrics like impressions, reach, engagement, and conversion rates.

Step 9: Optimize and Iterate

• Optimize Based on Results: Analyze performance metrics and audience feedback to refine future ad campaigns. Adjust targeting, messaging, or ad placement for better results.

Step 10: Compliance and Regulations

• Adhere to Regulations: Ensure compliance with local regulations, platform policies, and advertising standards when creating and distributing your audio ads.

By following these steps, you can create impactful and engaging audio ads that effectively convey your message, resonate with your target audience, and drive desired actions on various audio platforms.

STRATEGIES FOR EFFECTIVE AD PLACEMENT WITHOUT COMPROMISING USER EXPERIENCE

Ensuring effective ad placement without compromising user experience is essential for maintaining a positive relationship with your audience while optimizing revenue generation. Here are strategies to achieve this balance:

1. Understand User Behavior:

• User Flow Analysis: Analyze user behavior and navigation patterns on your website or platform to identify optimal ad placements without disrupting user flow.

• Heatmaps and Analytics: Utilize tools like heatmaps and website analytics to determine high-traffic areas and natural breakpoints for ad placement.

2. Balance Ad Density:

• Limit Ad Quantity: Avoid overcrowding pages with excessive ads. Maintain a balanced ratio of content to ads to prevent overwhelming users with promotional material.

• Strategic Ad Spacing: Space out ads throughout the content to create a visually appealing layout while allowing users to engage with the primary content.

3. Prioritize Above-the-Fold:

• Top-of-Page Placement: Place key ads (e.g., leaderboard or top-performing banner ads) above the fold for high visibility without requiring users to scroll immediately.

• Non-Intrusive Size: Use ad sizes that fit naturally within the top section of the page without dominating the entire screen.

4. In-Content Native Ads:

• Seamless Integration: Embed native ads within content, matching the style and format of the surrounding material to blend in organically.

• Relevance and Context: Ensure native ads are contextually relevant to the content they appear alongside, offering value to users.

5. Contextual Ad Placement:

• Relevant Placement: Display ads contextually relevant to the content, ensuring they complement the user's interests and browsing experience.

• Targeted Advertising: Utilize user data and targeting options to display ads that resonate with specific audience segments, increasing the likelihood of engagement.

6. Optimize Mobile Experience:

• Mobile-Friendly Ads: Ensure ads are responsive and optimized for mobile devices, fitting seamlessly within smaller screen sizes without hindering navigation.

• Strategic Mobile Placement: Place ads in areas that are visible and accessible on mobile screens without obstructing essential content or navigation.

7. A/B Testing and Iteration:

• Experiment with Placements: Conduct A/B tests to compare different ad placements, sizes, or formats, allowing data-driven decisions to optimize placements.

• Continuous Improvement: Based on performance data, iterate and refine ad placements to improve engagement without compromising user satisfaction.

8. Transparent Labeling and Disclosure:

• Clearly Label Ads: Clearly mark ads as "sponsored," "promoted," or "ad" to maintain transparency and avoid confusion between ad content and organic content.

• Non-Intrusive Disclosure: Integrate disclosure seamlessly without disrupting the user experience or content flow.

9. Respect User Experience:

• Page Load Speed: Optimize ad load times to ensure they don't significantly impact page load speed, preserving a smooth browsing experience.

• Ad Blocker Consideration: Respect users' preferences regarding ad blockers and offer valuable content that encourages them to consider disabling blockers.

Balancing effective ad placement with a positive user experience involves a delicate approach. By prioritizing relevance, strategic placement, and user-centricity, you can optimize ad performance while maintaining a seamless and engaging experience for your audience. Regularly monitoring user feedback and performance metrics will help fine-tune your ad placement strategies over time.

BEST PRACTICES FOR INTEGRATING THE DIFFERENT TYPES OF AD FORMAT WITHIN CONTENT

Integrating various ad formats within content requires a thoughtful approach to maintain a harmonious user experience while effectively delivering advertising messages. Here are best practices for integrating different ad formats within content:

1. Native Ads Integration:

• Relevance and Context: Ensure native ads seamlessly blend with the surrounding content, staying relevant and contextually aligned with the platform.

• Visual Consistency: Match the design elements of native ads with the platform's overall style, avoiding stark contrasts that might disrupt the user experience.

2. Display Ads Integration:

• Strategic Placement: Position display ads strategically within content, maintaining a balanced ratio between content and ads to prevent overwhelming users.

• Relevant Context: Display ads that are contextually relevant to the content they appear alongside, enhancing user engagement.

3. Video Ads Integration:

• In-Stream Video Placement: Integrate in-stream video ads at natural breakpoints or between content sections, avoiding abrupt interruptions.

• Seamless Transition: Ensure video ads flow naturally with the content, providing value or entertainment without disrupting the overall viewing experience.

4. Social Media Ads Integration:

• Harmonious Appearance: Create social media ads that match the style and tone of organic posts, ensuring they blend seamlessly into users' feeds.

• Engagement-Oriented Content: Craft social media ads that encourage interaction, conversation, or sharing, promoting engagement within the platform.

5. Mobile Ads Integration:

• Responsive Design: Develop mobile-friendly ad formats that adapt well to various screen sizes, maintaining readability and usability.

• Non-Intrusive Placement: Place mobile ads strategically, allowing easy access without hindering navigation or obstructing essential content.

6. Transparency and Disclosure:

• Clearly Label Ads: Label sponsored or promoted content clearly to maintain transparency and avoid confusing it with organic content.

• Non-Disruptive Disclosure: Integrate disclosure seamlessly without interrupting the user experience or content flow.

7. User-Centric Approach:

• Value-Oriented Content: Provide value to users through ads, whether it's informative, entertaining, or relevant, enhancing the overall user experience.

• User Feedback Consideration: Consider user feedback and behavior when optimizing ad integration, ensuring it aligns with user preferences.

8. Testing and Iteration:

• A/B Testing: Experiment with different placements, formats, or designs to identify what resonates best with the audience without compromising user satisfaction.

• Performance Monitoring: Continuously monitor performance metrics to refine and optimize ad integration strategies based on user engagement and conversions.

9. Ad Load Optimization:

• Balanced Ad Density: Avoid excessive ad placements that may overwhelm users. Balance ad frequency to maintain a positive user experience.

• Load Speed Optimization: Optimize ad loading times to prevent slowdowns in page or content loading, contributing to a smoother user experience.

By implementing these best practices, content creators and advertisers can effectively integrate various ad formats within content, optimizing user experience while achieving advertising objectives. Regular monitoring and refinement based on user feedback and performance metrics are crucial for sustained success in ad integration.

A/B TESTING PROCESS

A/B testing, also known as split testing, is a method used to compare two different versions of something, such as a webpage, an ad, or an app feature, to determine which one performs better. The goal of A/B testing is to understand user behavior, preferences, and interactions to optimize for better performance. Here is a detailed explanation of the A/B testing process:

A/B Testing Process:

1. Identify Objectives and Hypotheses:

• Define Goals: Clearly outline the objectives and key performance indicators (KPIs) you want to improve (e.g., click-through rate, conversion rate, engagement metrics).

• Formulate Hypotheses: Develop hypotheses about potential changes that could positively impact the chosen KPIs.

2. Define Testing Variables:

• Choose Elements to Test: Select a specific element or variable to test (e.g., headline, call-to-action, layout, color scheme).

• Create Variations: Develop two or more variations of the chosen element, such as Version A (control) and Version B (variation).

3. Test Implementation:

• Randomized Testing: Randomly assign users to different groups, presenting them with either Version A or Version B.

• Testing Duration: Run the test for a sufficient duration to collect a significant amount of data, considering factors like traffic volume and conversion rates.

4. Data Collection and Analysis:

• Collect Metrics: Measure and collect data on user interactions, performance metrics, and conversions for each version.

• Statistical Analysis: Analyze the collected data using statistical methods to determine the performance differences between versions.

5. Draw Conclusions:

• Evaluate Results: Compare the performance metrics of Version A and Version B against the predefined objectives and KPIs.

• Statistical Significance: Determine if the observed differences are statistically significant and not due to random chance.

6. Implement Better Performing Version:

• Choose Winning Variant: Implement the version that performed better based on the predefined goals and statistical significance.

• Apply Learnings: Apply the learnings from the test to future iterations or improvements.

7. Continuous Iteration:

• Iterative Testing: Use insights gained from A/B testing to continuously refine elements and iterate further tests for ongoing optimization.

• Regular Monitoring: Continuously monitor performance metrics and user behavior to identify new opportunities for testing and improvement.

Best Practices for A/B Testing:

• Focus on One Variable: Test a single element or variable at a time to clearly identify its impact on performance.

• Sufficient Sample Size: Ensure tests are conducted with a sufficiently large sample size to draw statistically significant conclusions.

• Randomization: Randomly assign users to different variations to eliminate bias and obtain reliable results.

• Clear Objectives: Clearly define objectives and metrics to measure success before conducting the test.

• Patience and Iteration: A/B testing is an iterative process; be patient and persistent in testing and refining elements for better results.

A/B testing provides valuable insights into user preferences and behavior, enabling data-driven decisions to optimize digital assets, improve user experience, and achieve desired outcomes effectively.

OPTIMIZATION TECHNIqUES

Optimization techniques refer to the strategies and methods used to improve the performance, efficiency, or effectiveness of systems, processes, websites, or digital assets. Here is a detailed explanation of optimization techniques:

1. Website Optimization:

Performance Optimization:

• Page Speed: Minimize load times by optimizing images, reducing server response time, and utilizing caching techniques.

- Mobile Optimization: Ensure responsiveness and usability on various devices by employing mobile-friendly design principles.

SEO Optimization:

- Keyword Optimization: Research and use relevant keywords in content, metadata, and headings to improve search engine visibility.

- Link Building: Acquire quality backlinks to improve domain authority and search rankings.

2. Conversion Rate Optimization (CRO):

- A/B Testing: Experiment with variations of elements like headlines, CTAs, or layouts to enhance conversion rates.

- User Experience (UX) Optimization: Improve navigation, usability, and clarity of information to encourage conversions.

3. Digital Advertising Optimization:

- Ad Targeting: Refine targeting options based on demographics, interests, or behavior to reach the most relevant audience.

- Ad Copy and Design Optimization: Test different ad creatives, messages, or visuals to determine the most effective combinations.

4. Content Optimization:

Content Quality Improvement:

• SEO-Optimized Content: Create valuable and engaging content optimized for search engines and user intent.

• Content Updates: Regularly update and improve existing content to maintain relevance and accuracy.

Visual and Multimedia Optimization:

• Rich Media Integration: Use high-quality images, videos, or infographics to enhance content appeal and user engagement.

• Visual Consistency: Maintain a consistent visual style across content for brand recognition.

5. Data-Driven Optimization:

Analytics Utilization:

• Performance Monitoring: Use analytics tools to track KPIs and user behavior, guiding optimization efforts.

• User Feedback Analysis: Gather and analyze user feedback to identify areas for improvement.

Iterative Improvement:

• Continuous Testing: Conduct ongoing A/B tests, iterate based on insights, and refine strategies for continuous improvement.

• Agile Methodology: Adopt agile principles to iterate quickly and adapt strategies based on changing trends or user needs.

6. User Experience (UX) Optimization:

Usability Enhancement:

• Usability Testing: Conduct tests to identify usability issues and make the interface more intuitive and user-friendly.

• Accessibility Improvements: Ensure compliance with accessibility standards to accommodate diverse user needs.

Personalization and Customization:

• Personalized Experiences: Tailor content, recommendations, or product offerings based on user preferences or behavior.

• User-Centric Design: Design interfaces and experiences centered around user needs and behaviors.

7. E-commerce Optimization:

Checkout Process Optimization:

• Streamlined Checkout: Simplify the checkout process to reduce cart abandonment rates.

• Payment Options: Offer diverse payment methods to accommodate customer preferences.

Product Page Optimization:

• Product Descriptions and Images: Enhance product information and visuals to improve user confidence and decision-making.

• User Reviews Integration: Display user reviews and ratings to build trust and credibility.

8. Email Marketing Optimization:

Personalization and Segmentation:

• Targeted Campaigns: Segment audiences and personalize email content to increase engagement and conversion rates.

• Subject Line Testing: Test different subject lines to optimize open rates.

9. Social Media Optimization:

Content Sharing Optimization:

• Engagement Strategies: Create shareable content and encourage user engagement through polls, contests, or interactive posts.

• Optimal Posting Times: Identify the best times to post content for maximum reach and engagement.

Key Considerations for Optimization:

• Data-Driven Approach: Base optimization decisions on data, analytics, and user feedback rather than assumptions.

• Iterative Approach: Continuously test, measure, and refine strategies for ongoing improvement.

• Cross-Functional Collaboration: Encourage collaboration between departments or teams to leverage diverse expertise for optimization efforts.

• User-Centricity: Prioritize user needs, preferences, and experiences in all optimization initiatives.

By employing these optimization techniques across various domains, businesses can improve performance, enhance user experiences, and achieve better outcomes in their respective areas of operation.

BEST PRACTICES FOR AD PLACEMENT ON WEBSITE

Optimizing ad placement on a website is crucial for balancing revenue generation with a positive user experience. Here are best practices for ad placement:

1. Prioritize User Experience:

• Page Load Speed: Ensure ads don't significantly slow down the page load times, impacting user experience.

- Non-Intrusive Design: Place ads strategically without obstructing or distracting users from content consumption.

2. Strategic Placement:

- Above-the-Fold: Position key ads above the fold for immediate visibility without requiring users to scroll.

- Natural Breakpoints: Insert ads at natural content breakpoints (e.g., between sections or paragraphs) to maintain content flow.

3. Responsive Design:

- Mobile Optimization: Ensure ad placements are optimized for mobile devices to maintain readability and usability.

- Adaptability: Use responsive ad units that adjust to various screen sizes for consistency across devices.

4. Blend with Content:

- Native Ad Integration: Embed ads that seamlessly blend with content, matching the design and style of the website.

- Relevance: Display ads that are contextually relevant to the surrounding content for better user engagement.

5. Test and Monitor Performance:

- A/B Testing: Experiment with different ad placements, sizes, or formats to identify high-performing configurations.

• Performance Analytics: Continuously monitor ad performance metrics to refine placements and optimize for better results.

6. Respect Ad Density:

• Balanced Ad Quantity: Avoid overcrowding pages with too many ads; maintain a balance between content and advertisements.

• Ad Space Utilization: Utilize white space effectively, ensuring ads don't overpower or clutter the page.

7. Consider User Behavior:

• Eye-Tracking Studies: Use data or studies on user behavior to place ads where users are more likely to focus their attention.

• Heatmaps and Analytics: Analyze user heatmaps and behavior flow to determine optimal ad placements.

8. Clear Labeling and Transparency:

• Disclosure of Ads: Clearly label ads as "sponsored," "ad," or "promoted" to maintain transparency with users.

• Non-Intrusive Disclosure: Integrate disclosure seamlessly without disrupting the user experience.

9. Ad Blocker Consideration:

• Appeal to Users: Offer value and non-intrusive ad experiences to encourage users to reconsider using ad blockers.

• Diverse Revenue Streams: Explore alternative revenue sources beyond ads to reduce reliance on ad revenue alone.

10. Adherence to Policies:

• Compliance with Guidelines: Ensure ad placements comply with ad network policies and industry standards.

• Quality Control: Regularly review and monitor ad content to maintain high-quality standards and relevance.

By following these best practices, website owners and publishers can optimize ad placement to balance revenue generation with a positive user experience, fostering user engagement while ensuring compliance with industry standards and user expectations. Regular monitoring, testing, and optimization are essential for sustained success in ad placement.

Ad placement on blogs should aim to generate revenue while maintaining a positive user experience. Here are best practices for ad placement on blogs:

1. Understand User Experience:

• Balance Content and Ads: Maintain a balance between ads and content to avoid overwhelming users with ads.

• Non-Intrusive Placement: Place ads strategically without obstructing or distracting readers from the main content.

2. Native and Contextual Integration:

• Seamless Integration: Integrate native ads that blend with the blog's theme, style, and content flow.

• Relevance: Display ads that are contextually relevant to the blog content and audience interests.

3. Prioritize User Engagement:

• Above-the-Fold: Position key ads, like banner ads or native banners, above the fold for immediate visibility.

• In-Content Ads: Place ads within the content at natural breakpoints, maintaining the reading flow.

4. Responsive and Mobile Optimization:

• Responsive Design: Ensure ad placements are optimized for various screen sizes and devices.

• Mobile-Friendly: Prioritize mobile optimization to maintain readability and usability on smaller screens.

5. Test and Monitor Performance:

• A/B Testing: Experiment with different ad placements, sizes, or formats to identify high-performing configurations.

• Performance Analytics: Monitor ad performance metrics regularly to refine placements and optimize for better results.

6. Clear Labeling and Transparency:

• Disclosure of Ads: Clearly label ads as "sponsored," "ad," or "promoted" to maintain transparency.

• Non-Intrusive Disclosure: Integrate disclosure seamlessly without disrupting the reading experience.

7. Respect User Behavior:

• User Behavior Analysis: Analyze reader behavior to determine optimal ad placements based on user engagement.

• Heatmaps and Analytics: Utilize data on user behavior and heatmaps to optimize ad placements.

8. Optimal Ad Density:

• Balanced Quantity: Avoid excessive ad placements; maintain a balance to preserve the blog's readability and aesthetic.

• Ad Space Utilization: Utilize white space effectively, ensuring ads complement rather than overwhelm the content.

9. Quality Content and User Engagement:

• Content Priority: Prioritize quality content over excessive ad placements to retain and engage readers.

• Engagement Focus: Aim for ad placements that encourage user interaction without disrupting their experience.

10. Compliance with Policies:

• Ad Network Guidelines: Ensure compliance with ad network policies and industry standards.

• Quality Assurance: Regularly review and monitor ad content to maintain high-quality standards and relevance.

11. Ad Blocker Consideration:

• Appeal to Users: Offer non-intrusive ad experiences to encourage users to reconsider using ad blockers.

• Diverse Revenue Streams: Explore alternative revenue sources beyond ads to reduce reliance on ad revenue alone.

By adhering to these best practices, bloggers can effectively place ads on their blogs, optimizing revenue while ensuring a positive user experience and compliance with industry standards. Regularly analyzing user behavior and testing different ad placements are essential for ongoing optimization.

BEST PRACTICES FOR AD PLACEMENT ON VIDEOS

When placing ads within videos, whether on platforms like YouTube or embedded on websites, it's essential to strike a balance between monetization and providing a seamless viewing experience. Here are best practices for ad placement on videos:

1. Consider User Experience:

• Non-Intrusive Placement: Integrate ads at natural breaks to avoid disrupting the viewing experience.

• Frequency Cap: Limit the number of ads shown to prevent overwhelming viewers with interruptions.

2. Ad Format Variety:

• Skippable Ads: Offer skippable ads when possible to give viewers control and reduce frustration.

• Non-Skippable Ads: Use sparingly for shorter content or at strategic points to maintain engagement.

3. Pre-Roll, Mid-Roll, and Post-Roll Ads:

• Pre-Roll Ads: Place ads before the video starts, keeping them short and engaging to retain viewer attention.

• Mid-Roll Ads: Insert ads during longer videos at natural breakpoints, like pauses in the content.

• Post-Roll Ads: Display ads after the video ends without disrupting the core content.

4. Native and Contextual Ads:

• Native Integration: Integrate branded or sponsored content that aligns naturally with the video theme and style.

• Contextual Relevance: Display ads relevant to the video content to increase engagement and resonance.

5. Interactive and Engaging Ads:

• Interactive Elements: Include interactive elements like polls or links in ads to engage viewers.

• Call-to-Action (CTA): Encourage actions through clear and compelling CTAs within or after the ad.

6. Ad Length and Placement:

• Ad Duration: Keep ad lengths reasonable and relevant to the video length to maintain user interest.

- Strategic Placement: Experiment with different ad placements and lengths to optimize user engagement.

7. Personalization and Targeting:

- Audience Segmentation: Use targeting options to serve relevant ads based on viewer demographics or preferences.

- Behavioral Targeting: Tailor ads based on user behavior or past interactions for better relevance.

8. Test and Analyze:

- A/B Testing: Experiment with different ad formats, placements, and lengths to identify what works best.

- Performance Metrics: Analyze engagement metrics and user feedback to refine ad placement strategies.

9. Transparency and User Choice:

- Disclosure and Transparency: Clearly label ads as "sponsored," "promoted," or "ad" to maintain transparency.

- Viewer Choice: Provide options whenever possible, like the ability to skip or control ad frequency.

10. Compliance and Quality:

- Ad Guidelines: Adhere to platform guidelines and standards to ensure compliance and quality.

• Regular Monitoring: Monitor ad content and performance to ensure it aligns with standards and viewer expectations.

By implementing these best practices, content creators and platforms can effectively integrate ads within videos to generate revenue while ensuring a positive and engaging viewing experience for users. Regularly analyzing data and user behavior is crucial for refining ad placement strategies.

HOW TO BALANCE USER EXPERIENCE WITH AD VISIBILITY

Balancing user experience with Ad visibility is essential to ensure that users have a positive experience while still allowing ads to be visible and effective. Here are strategies to strike a balance:

1. Opt for Non-Intrusive Ad Formats:

• Native Ads: Integrate ads seamlessly into the content, matching the style and tone of the platform to avoid disrupting the user experience.

• In-Feed Ads: Place ads within content feeds in a way that aligns with the platform's natural flow, without interrupting the user's browsing.

2. Consider Ad Placement:

• Strategic Placement: Position ads at natural breakpoints, such as between sections or paragraphs, to maintain content flow.

• Above-the-Fold: Place key ads within the initial visible screen space to ensure visibility without requiring users to scroll immediately.

3. Limit Ad Density:

• Balanced Ad Quantity: Avoid overcrowding pages or content with too many ads to prevent overwhelming users.

• Whitespace Utilization: Allow for ample whitespace around ads to prevent clutter and maintain a clean layout.

4. Optimize Ad Loading:

• Page Load Speed: Ensure ads don't significantly impact page load times, preserving a seamless and fast browsing experience.

• Lazy Loading: Implement techniques like lazy loading to prioritize content and load ads only as they come into view.

5. Prioritize User Control:

• Ad Customization: Offer users options to personalize or control their ad experience, such as opting out of certain ad categories.

• Skip Options: Provide users with the ability to skip or close ads after a reasonable duration.

6. Ad Relevance and Transparency:

• Relevant Ads: Display ads that are contextually relevant to the content or user's interests, enhancing engagement.

• Disclosure and Transparency: Clearly label ads as "sponsored," "ad," or "promoted" to maintain transparency with users.

7. Test and Analyze:

• User Feedback: Collect feedback and monitor user behavior to understand their preferences regarding ad visibility.

• A/B Testing: Experiment with different ad placements and formats to identify what resonates best with users.

8. Focus on Quality:

• High-Quality Content: Prioritize quality content and user experience over excessive ad placements for long-term user retention.

• Ad Quality Assurance: Regularly review and ensure ad content meets quality standards to maintain a positive perception.

9. Comply with Guidelines:

• Ad Network Policies: Adhere to ad network guidelines and industry standards to ensure compliance and quality.

• User Data Privacy: Respect user privacy and comply with data protection regulations while targeting ads.

By implementing these strategies, content creators and advertisers can balance ad visibility with a positive user experience, ensuring that users engage with the content and ads effectively without feeling overwhelmed or disrupted. Regularly assessing user feedback and refining strategies accordingly is crucial for long-term success.

CHAPTER FOUR

THE ADSENSE DASHBOARD

The AdSense dashboard provides an interface where publishers can monitor, analyze, and manage their AdSense account, ad performance, earnings, and various metrics. Here's a breakdown of the key elements typically found in the AdSense dashboard:

1. Overview Section:

• Earnings Overview: A snapshot of your earnings for the selected timeframe, displaying total revenue, estimated earnings, RPM (Revenue per thousand impressions), and other key financial metrics.

• Performance Graphs: Graphical representation of earnings, clicks, impressions, and other metrics over time, allowing for easy visualization of performance trends.

2. Performance Reports:

• Date Range Selector: Allows you to choose the timeframe for which you want to view performance data.

• Metrics: Offers various metrics like page views, clicks, RPM, CPC (Cost Per Click), CTR (Click-Through Rate), and earnings, providing insights into ad performance.

• Ad Units/Custom Channels: Breakdown of performance metrics by individual ad units or custom channels for tracking specific ad placements or segments.

3. Payment Section:

• Payments Overview: Information related to your payments, including current balance, earnings, payment history, and payment settings.

• Payment Threshold: Allows you to set a threshold for when you'll receive payment, based on your earnings.

4. Blocking Controls:

• Ad Review Center: Provides options to review and manage ad categories, allowing you to block or allow specific types of ads from appearing on your site.

• Simplified Ad Blocking: Enables publishers to block sensitive categories or specific ad categories from displaying on their websites.

5. Alerts and Notifications:

• Policy Notifications: Alerts about any policy violations or issues related to your account or ad placements.

• Payment Notifications: Updates about payment processing, thresholds, or payment-related issues.

6. Optimization and Recommendations:

• Optimization Tips: Suggestions and recommendations from AdSense to improve ad performance, user experience, or revenue.

• Experiments and Tests: Offers options to conduct A/B tests or experiments on ad placements for better performance.

7. Help and Resources:

• Support and Help Center: Direct links to AdSense help articles, community forums, or support channels for assistance and troubleshooting.

8. Additional Features (Varies Based on Account):

• Ad Formats: Information on various ad formats available and their performance metrics.

• Sites/URLs: Data breakdown by specific websites or URLs where ads are displayed.

Navigation and Customization:

• Menu and Filters: Navigation menu to access different sections like Ads, Sites, Reports, Payments, etc.

• Customization Options: Ability to customize the dashboard layout, metrics displayed, and report settings for personalized tracking.

Please note that the AdSense dashboard might have received updates or undergone changes after my last update. Users should refer to the most recent interface and resources provided by AdSense for accurate and detailed information.

REPORTING TOOLS

Reporting tools in AdSense offer publishers detailed insights into their ad performance, earnings, and various metrics. These tools empower users to analyze data, track trends, and make informed decisions to optimize revenue. Here's an in-depth look at reporting tools typically available in AdSense:

1. Performance Reports:

• Date Range Selection: Allows customization of the timeframe to analyze performance data.

• Metrics: Provides a wide range of performance metrics such as clicks, impressions, RPM (Revenue per thousand impressions), CPC (Cost Per Click), CTR (Click-Through Rate), earnings, and more.

• Dimension Breakdown: Offers segmentation options to break down data by ad units, ad sizes, ad types, custom channels, sites, countries, and other dimensions for detailed analysis.

• Graphical Representation: Presents data in graphical formats like line graphs, bar charts, and pie charts for visualizing trends and patterns.

2. Custom Channels and URL Reports:

• Custom Channel Performance: Detailed insights into the performance of specific ad placements or groups created using custom channels.

• URL Performance: Breakdown of ad performance metrics by individual websites or URLs where ads are displayed.

3. Ad Units Reports:

• Ad Unit Analysis: Information on how different ad units perform, helping identify which placements generate the most revenue or engagement.

4. Site Reports:

• Site-Level Performance: Data breakdown by specific websites or domains, allowing publishers to track performance across different sites.

5. Ad Formats and Sizes Reports:

• Ad Format Performance: Metrics based on different ad formats like display ads, text ads, native ads, etc., to determine the most effective formats.

• Ad Size Analysis: Insights into how various ad sizes perform in terms of user engagement and revenue generation.

6. Advanced Filtering and Comparison:

• Filtering Options: Advanced filtering capabilities to refine reports based on specific criteria such as date, device, geography, or user demographics.

• Comparison Tools: Allows comparison of metrics between different dimensions or timeframes for better analysis and decision-making.

7. Export and Data Sharing:

• Export Reports: Ability to export reports in various formats (CSV, PDF, etc.) for further analysis or sharing with stakeholders.

• Scheduled Reports: Option to schedule and receive reports automatically via email at specified intervals.

8. Real-Time Reporting:

• Real-Time Data: Provides insights into current ad performance, allowing publishers to monitor metrics as they happen.

9. Optimization Suggestions:

• Recommendations and Tips: Insights or suggestions provided by AdSense to optimize ad placements, formats, or strategies based on performance data.

10. Help and Support:

• Help Documentation: Access to help articles, tutorials, and guides within the reporting interface for assistance.

• Support Resources: Links to support forums, community boards, or direct customer support channels for further assistance.

These reporting tools offer publishers comprehensive data and analytics to assess ad performance, track revenue, and optimize strategies for better results. Users can customize reports, drill down into specific metrics, and derive actionable insights to improve their Ad monetization strategies.

HOW TO UTILIZE FEATURES LIKE CUSTOM CHANNELS, URL CHANNELS, ETC., FOR BETTER INSIGHTS

Features like Custom Channels and URL Channels in Google AdSense can significantly enhance insights into ad performance by providing more granular data and control over tracking. Here's how to leverage these features effectively:

1. Custom Channels:

Custom Channels allow publishers to group ad units based on specific criteria, enabling better tracking and analysis of ad performance within AdSense. Here's how to use them:

• Purpose: Create custom channels to categorize ad units by location, format, size, or any criteria relevant to your site's structure.

• Insights: Gain insights into how different ad groups perform in terms of clicks, impressions, CTR, and earnings, facilitating comparisons between various placements.

• Optimization: Identify high-performing ad placements or formats by comparing custom channels, enabling better optimization strategies.

2. URL Channels:

URL Channels enable publishers to track performance metrics for specific websites or individual pages where ads are displayed. Here's how to utilize them effectively:

• Granular Tracking: Add individual URLs or entire domains to track performance metrics at a granular level.

• Site-Level Insights: Monitor how different sites or pages contribute to ad revenue, allowing optimizations based on specific URLs' performance.

• Content Analysis: Understand which pages or sections of your website generate more revenue or engagement, aiding content strategy and ad placement decisions.

3. Implementation Tips:

• Strategic Grouping: Plan and organize custom channels based on logical groupings that align with your site's layout or ad placement strategy.

• Detailed URL Tracking: Add URLs relevant to specific sections or high-traffic pages to get more accurate insights into their performance.

• Regular Review: Periodically review and analyze data from custom and URL channels to identify trends and optimize ad placements for better performance.

4. Optimization Strategies:

• Identify High Performers: Identify top-performing ad placements or specific pages that generate more revenue to replicate success across your site.

• Testing and Iteration: Use insights from custom and URL channels to conduct A/B tests or experiment with different ad formats/placements for optimization.

5. Reporting and Analysis:

• Reporting Insights: Leverage reporting tools in AdSense to analyze data from custom and URL channels, comparing performance metrics and deriving actionable insights.

• Data-driven Decisions: Base decisions regarding ad placements, content strategies, or optimizations on the data obtained from these channels.

By effectively utilizing Custom Channels and URL Channels in AdSense, publishers can gain deeper insights into ad performance, identify areas for improvement, and optimize their strategies to maximize ad revenue and user engagement. Regular monitoring and strategic adjustments based on these insights are key to success.

A/B TESTING STRATEGIES FOR AD SIZES, AD PLACEMENT AND AD FORMATS

When conducting A/B tests for Ad sizes and Ad placement, the goal is to determine which size generates higher engagement, click-through rates (CTR), conversions, and overall revenue. Here are effective strategies for A/B testing different ad sizes:

1. Define Clear Objectives:

• Set Goals: Clearly define what you aim to achieve through the A/B test—whether it's increased CTR, improved user engagement, higher conversions, or better revenue generation.

2. Selecting Ad Sizes for Testing:

• Variety of Sizes: Choose two or more different ad sizes to compare their performance. For example, compare a leaderboard (728x90) with a rectangle (300x250).

• Consider Placement: Test sizes that fit well within your website layout and user experience without being too intrusive.

Selecting Ad Placements for Testing:

• Variety of Placements: Choose multiple locations on your website for ad placement testing. For instance, compare between above-the-fold, sidebar, in-content, or footer placements.

• Consider User Experience: Test placements that maintain a good user experience without being intrusive or disrupting content consumption.

Selecting Ad Formats for Testing:

• Choose Variants: Select two or more ad formats to test against each other. For instance, compare display ads versus native ads, or different sizes of the same format.

• Consider Context: Ensure the ad formats align with your content and audience preferences to provide relevant comparisons.

3. Test Duration and Sample Size:

• Adequate Duration: Run the test for a sufficient period, usually a few weeks, to collect significant data that accurately represents performance variations.

• Statistically Significant Sample: Ensure the test runs long enough to accommodate fluctuations in traffic and provide statistically significant results.

4. Implementing the A/B Test:

• Randomized Display: Randomly display different ad sizes to users visiting your site to avoid biased results.

• Single Variable Testing: Test only one variable (ad size) at a time to accurately determine its impact on performance.

5. Tracking and Measurement:

• Key Metrics: Define the key performance indicators (KPIs) you want to track, such as CTR, conversion rate, revenue per thousand impressions (RPM), or overall earnings.

• Implement Tracking: Use tracking parameters or UTM tags to differentiate between the ad size variants in your analytics platform.

6. Analyzing Results:

• Statistical Significance: Ensure that the sample size is sufficient to yield statistically significant results.

• Comparison of Metrics: Analyze performance metrics across different ad sizes to identify which size performs better based on your defined objectives.

7. Implementing Winning Variants:

• Implement Changes: Deploy the winning ad size based on the performance results to replace the underperforming variant.

• Continuous Optimization: Use insights gained from the A/B test to continuously refine strategies and improve ad performance.

8. Continuous Testing and Iteration:

• Iterative Approach: A/B testing is an ongoing process. Once a test is completed, consider testing other ad size variations to further optimize performance.

9. Platform Compliance:

• Adherence to Policies: Ensure that all ad sizes used in the A/B tests comply with platform policies and guidelines.

10. Monitor and Adapt:

• Regular Monitoring: Continuously monitor ad performance even after implementing changes to detect any shifts or fluctuations.

• Adaptation: Be ready to adapt and conduct further tests as user behaviors or preferences evolve.

By applying these strategies, publishers can conduct effective A/B tests for different ad sizes, platforms and formats, enabling data-driven decisions to optimize their ad strategies and maximize revenue. Regular testing and analysis are crucial for staying updated with changing user preferences and industry trends.

SEO TECHNIqUES TO BOOST TRAFFIC AND AD REVENUE

To increase website traffic and subsequently improve ad revenue, employing effective Search Engine Optimization (SEO) techniques is crucial. Here are some strategies to boost traffic and enhance ad revenue through SEO:

1. Keyword Research and Optimization:

• Keyword Analysis: Identify relevant and high-traffic keywords related to your content and niche using tools like Google Keyword Planner, SEMrush, or Ahrefs.

• Optimized Content: Create high-quality, informative, and engaging content that incorporates targeted keywords naturally while maintaining readability.

• Title Tags and Meta Descriptions: Craft compelling and keyword-rich titles and meta descriptions to improve click-through rates from search engine results pages (SERPs).

2. Content Quality and Freshness:

• High-Quality Content: Publish authoritative, comprehensive, and original content that addresses user queries or needs, making it valuable and shareable.

• Regular Updates: Keep content updated and fresh by revising and adding new information, which can improve search ranking and user engagement.

3. On-Page SEO:

• Optimize Site Structure: Ensure easy navigation and a clear site structure for both users and search engines, using appropriate headings, URLs, and internal linking.

• Mobile Optimization: Create a responsive design that works seamlessly across various devices, prioritizing mobile-friendliness for better rankings.

4. Technical SEO:

• Page Speed Optimization: Improve site speed by compressing images, enabling browser caching, and utilizing content delivery networks (CDNs) to enhance user experience and SEO rankings.

• Schema Markup: Implement structured data markup to help search engines understand your content better and display rich snippets in search results.

5. Backlink Building:

• Quality Backlinks: Earn or build authoritative and relevant backlinks from reputable websites in your industry, as they positively impact your site's authority and search rankings.

• Guest Posting and Outreach: Engage in guest posting on relevant sites or outreach campaigns to acquire backlinks from high-quality sources.

6. User Experience (UX) Enhancement:

• Improved UX Design: Focus on user-friendly design, intuitive navigation, and clear call-to-actions (CTAs) to enhance user experience, reducing bounce rates and increasing user engagement.

7. Analyze and Adapt:

• Monitor Analytics: Regularly analyze website performance metrics using tools like Google Analytics to track traffic sources, user behavior, and ad performance.

• Experiment and Optimize: Use data-driven insights to experiment with different strategies and optimize your SEO tactics continuously.

8. Local SEO Optimization:

• Local Listings: If applicable, optimize for local search by claiming and optimizing your Google My Business profile and local directories to attract local traffic.

9. Video and Image Optimization:

• Multimedia Optimization: Optimize videos and images by using relevant keywords in filenames, titles, alt text, and descriptions to improve visibility in image and video search results.

10. Social Media Integration:

• Social Sharing: Encourage social sharing of content to increase visibility and reach, potentially driving more traffic to your website.

By implementing these SEO strategies consistently and focusing on providing valuable and user-centric content, you can improve your website's visibility in search engines, attract more organic traffic, and subsequently enhance your ad revenue potential. Remember, SEO is an ongoing process that requires continuous monitoring, adaptation, and optimization.

TIPS ON INCREASING AD REVENUE THROUGH OPTIMIZATION AND TARGETED CONTENT CREATION

Increasing Ad revenue through optimization and targeted content creation involves various strategies focused on maximizing the value of your content and ad placements. Here are tips to help boost ad revenue:

1. Audience Research and Targeting:

• Understand Audience Needs: Conduct thorough research to comprehend your audience's interests, preferences, and behavior to create content tailored to their needs.

• Audience Segmentation: Segment your audience based on demographics, interests, and behaviors to deliver more targeted and relevant content and ads.

2. Quality Content Creation:

• High-Quality and Engaging Content: Produce valuable, informative, and engaging content that resonates with your audience's interests and encourages longer on-site engagement.

• Evergreen Content: Create evergreen content that remains relevant over time, driving continuous traffic and ad revenue.

3. Optimal Ad Placement and Formats:

• Strategic Ad Placement: Experiment with various ad placements (above the fold, in-content, sidebar, etc.) and identify the most effective locations that balance user experience and revenue generation.

• Diversified Ad Formats: Test different ad formats (display ads, native ads, video ads) to determine which ones perform best with your audience and content.

4. A/B Testing and Optimization:

• Continuous Testing: Conduct A/B tests for ad placements, formats, and content variations to identify what resonates best with your audience and yields higher ad revenue.

• Optimization for Performance: Use analytics data to optimize ad placements, formats, and content based on user behavior, click-through rates, and conversion metrics.

5. Responsive Design and User Experience:

• Mobile Optimization: Ensure your website and ads are mobile-responsive to cater to users accessing content from various devices, enhancing user experience and ad visibility.

- User-Friendly Experience: Prioritize user experience by creating a clean and easy-to-navigate website, reducing ad fatigue, and enhancing engagement.

6. SEO and Traffic Generation:

- SEO Strategies: Implement effective SEO techniques to improve organic traffic, as higher traffic volumes can positively impact ad revenue potential.

- Content Promotion: Promote your content across various channels (social media, email newsletters, etc.) to drive more traffic to your site and increase ad impressions.

7. Diversify Revenue Streams:

- Explore Alternative Monetization: Besides display ads, consider additional revenue streams like affiliate marketing, sponsored content, memberships, or selling digital products.

8. Advertiser Partnerships and Direct Sales:

- Direct Ad Sales: Explore direct ad sales or partnerships with advertisers relevant to your niche to secure higher-paying and more targeted ad placements.

9. Advertiser-Friendly Environment:

- Quality Assurance: Ensure your content aligns with ad network policies and maintains a brand-safe environment for advertisers, potentially attracting higher-paying campaigns.

10. Monitor Analytics and Iterate:

• Regular Monitoring and Analysis: Continuously track ad performance metrics, user behavior, and revenue analytics to identify trends and make data-driven decisions for further optimization.

By implementing these strategies, content creators can enhance their ad revenue by delivering targeted, high-quality content while optimizing ad placements and formats to cater to their audience's preferences and behaviors. Regularly testing, analyzing, and optimizing strategies based on data insights is key to maximizing ad revenue potential.

WHAT IS RPM?

RPM stands for "Revenue per Mille" or "Revenue per Thousand Impressions." It is a metric used in online advertising to measure the estimated earnings generated by a publisher for every thousand ad impressions served on their website or platform.

Formula for Calculating RPM:

The formula for calculating RPM is:

• RPM=RevenueNumber of Impressions×1000RPM=Number of ImpressionsRevenue×1000

• Revenue: Total earnings generated from ads displayed on a website or platform within a specific timeframe.

• Number of Impressions: The total count of ad impressions served within the same timeframe.

Key Points about RPM:

• Revenue Estimation: RPM is an estimation of how much a publisher earns per thousand ad impressions. It represents the publisher's ad revenue, not the advertisers spend.

• Comparison Metric: RPM allows publishers to compare the revenue performance of different pages, ad placements, or time periods, providing insights into which segments generate higher earnings.

• Performance Indicator: It serves as a performance indicator for publishers, helping them understand the effectiveness of their ad strategies and content monetization.

• Insight into Ad Performance: A higher RPM indicates better monetization efficiency, implying that the ads served are more relevant, engaging, or placed strategically to attract higher-paying advertisers.

Factors Influencing RPM:

• Ad Format and Placement: Certain ad formats or placements might generate higher RPMs due to better visibility and engagement.

• Content Quality: High-quality, targeted content often attracts more valuable ads and higher-paying advertisers, resulting in higher RPMs.

• Audience and Geographical Factors: Demographics, audience engagement, and geographic location can influence the RPM as advertisers might bid differently for various audience segments.

Limitations:

• Varied Revenue Models: RPM may not account for different revenue models (CPC, CPM, CPA) used in advertising.

• Not Sole Indicator: While RPM is valuable, it should be considered alongside other metrics like CTR, fill rate, and eCPM for a comprehensive understanding of ad performance.

Interpreting RPM:

• Comparative Analysis: Compare RPM across different pages, sections, or timeframes to identify high-performing areas and optimize lower-performing ones.

• Optimization Tool: Use RPM as a benchmark to optimize ad placements, content strategies, and user experience to improve overall revenue potential.

RPM is a valuable metric for publishers to evaluate their ad revenue performance and make informed decisions regarding content, ad placements, and optimization strategies to maximize their earnings.

WHAT IS CPC?

CPC stands for "Cost Per Click." It is a common metric used in online advertising to measure the cost an advertiser pays for a single click on their advertisement. CPC is an essential metric for advertisers, as it directly relates to the effectiveness and cost-efficiency of their advertising campaigns.

How CPC is Calculated:

The formula for calculating CPC is straightforward:

- CPC=Total CostNumber of ClicksCPC=Number of ClicksTotal Cost

• Total Cost: The total amount spent by the advertiser on a specific ad campaign or set of clicks within a defined time frame.

• Number of Clicks: The total count of clicks received on the ad during the same time frame.

Key Points about CPC:

• Performance Measurement: CPC measures the effectiveness of an ad campaign by determining the actual cost an advertiser incurs for each click on their ad.

• Bid Strategy: In systems like Google Ads, advertisers often set their maximum CPC bid, which is the highest amount they are willing to pay for a single click on their ad. The actual CPC can be lower than the maximum bid.

• Competitive Landscape: The CPC value can fluctuate based on competition, demand for keywords, ad relevance, and the quality of the Ad campaign. Highly competitive keywords or industries tend to have higher CPCs.

Factors Influencing CPC:

• Ad Relevance and Quality: Relevant and high-quality ads often achieve better click-through rates and lower CPCs.

• Keyword Competition: Highly competitive keywords might have higher CPCs due to increased bidding from advertisers.

• Ad Placement and Position: Ad placements in prime positions, such as top positions on search engine results pages (SERPs), might command higher CPCs.

• Target Audience and Geographical Factors: CPC can vary based on the audience's location, demographics, and device preferences.

• Revenue Model: CPC is commonly associated with pay-per-click (PPC) advertising models, where advertisers only pay when a user clicks on their ad.

• Ad Optimization: Advertisers often aim to optimize their ads and landing pages to improve relevancy, click-through rates, and conversions, thereby reducing the CPC and maximizing return on investment (ROI).

Interpreting CPC:

• Campaign Performance: Assess the performance of advertising campaigns by analyzing CPC alongside other metrics like CTR, conversion rates, and ROI.

• Budget Allocation: Determine the cost-effectiveness of ad spend and allocate budgets strategically based on CPC performance across different campaigns or keywords.

CPC is a critical metric for advertisers to gauge the efficiency and cost-effectiveness of their advertising efforts. By monitoring CPC and optimizing ad campaigns based on its performance, advertisers can maximize the effectiveness of their advertising budgets and achieve their desired goals more efficiently.

THE OTHER REVENUE METRICS

In addition to RPM (Revenue per Thousand Impressions) and CPC (Cost Per Click), there are several other important revenue metrics used in online advertising and digital marketing. Here's a detailed explanation of some key revenue metrics:

1. eCPM (Effective Cost Per Mille):

• Definition: eCPM represents the estimated earnings generated for every thousand ad impressions, regardless of the pricing model (CPC, CPM, CPA).

• Calculation: eCPM is calculated to provide a standardized comparison of ad revenue across different pricing models:

$$eCPM = \frac{Total\ Earnings}{Total\ Impressions} \times 1000$$

• Purpose: It helps publishers compare the revenue potential of various ad formats, placements, or networks, allowing them to optimize for higher eCPM areas.

2. Fill Rate:

• Definition: Fill rate indicates the percentage of ad inventory that is successfully filled with ads and monetized out of the total available ad inventory.

• Calculation: Fill Rate is calculated as:

$$Fill\ Rate = \frac{Ad\ Requests\ Filled}{Total\ Ad\ Requests} \times 100$$

• Importance: A high fill rate implies better Ad inventory monetization, while a low fill rate might indicate unmet demand or optimization opportunities.

3. CTR (Click-Through Rate):

• Definition: CTR measures the percentage of ad clicks compared to the total number of ad impressions served. It indicates how well an ad engages users.

• Calculation: CTR is calculated as:

$$CTR = \frac{Clicks}{Impressions} \times 100 \quad CTR = \frac{Clicks}{Impressions} \times 100$$

• Significance: A higher CTR often indicates a more compelling and relevant ad to users, contributing to increased ad performance and potentially higher revenue.

4. Conversion Rate:

• Definition: Conversion Rate measures the percentage of users who complete a desired action (e.g., purchase, sign-up) after clicking on an ad or visiting a website.

• Calculation: Conversion Rate is calculated as:

$$\text{Conversion Rate} = \frac{\text{Number of Conversions}}{\text{Number of Clicks}} \times 100 \quad \text{Conversion Rate} = \frac{\text{Number of Conversions}}{\text{Number of Clicks}} \times 100$$

• Importance: Higher conversion rates indicate better alignment between ad messaging and user expectations, leading to improved revenue generation.

5. ROI (Return on Investment):

• Definition: ROI measures the profitability of an advertising campaign by comparing the generated revenue against the advertising costs.

• Calculation: ROI is calculated as:

$$ROI = (Revenue - CostCost) \times 100 ROI = (CostRevenue - Cost) \times 100$$

• Significance: Positive ROI indicates profitability, while a negative ROI suggests that the campaign's costs exceed the revenue generated.

These metrics provide insights into different aspects of advertising performance and revenue generation. By analyzing and optimizing these metrics, advertisers and publishers can make data-driven decisions to enhance ad performance, increase revenue, and maximize return on investment.

CHAPTER FIVE

STRATEGIES FOR CREATING ADSENSE-FRIENDLY CONTENT

Creating AdSense-friendly content involves producing high-quality, original, and valuable content that complies with AdSense policies while maximizing revenue potential. Here are strategies for creating AdSense-friendly content:

1. Adherence to AdSense Policies:

• Policy Compliance: Familiarize yourself with AdSense program policies and guidelines to ensure your content meets their requirements, avoiding violations that could lead to account issues.

2. Valuable and Engaging Content:

• Quality Content: Focus on creating high-quality, original, and informative content that adds value to users and encourages engagement.

• User Intent Alignment: Understand user search intent and provide relevant, comprehensive content that answers their queries or addresses their needs.

3. Originality and Uniqueness:

• Avoid Plagiarism: Produce original content, avoiding duplicate or copied material to maintain authenticity and credibility.

• Unique Perspective: Offer unique insights, viewpoints, or angles on topics to stand out in a crowded content landscape.

4. Audience Relevance and Engagement:

• Target Audience Alignment: Create content tailored to your audience's interests, preferences, and demographics, ensuring relevance and engagement.

• Interactive Elements: Include engaging elements like videos, images, infographics, or interactive features to captivate users and enhance dwell time.

5. Readability and Accessibility:

• Clear Structure: Organize content with headings, subheadings, bullet points, and concise paragraphs for easy readability and navigation.

• Mobile Compatibility: Ensure content is mobile-friendly, as a significant portion of users accesses content via mobile devices.

6. SEO Best Practices:

• Keyword Optimization: Integrate relevant keywords naturally within your content to enhance search visibility without keyword stuffing.

• Meta Tags and Descriptions: Craft descriptive and engaging meta tags and descriptions for better SERP visibility.

7. Brand-Safe Environment:

• Avoid Controversial Topics: Steer clear of sensitive or controversial subjects that might negatively impact advertiser sentiment and brand safety.

8. Regular Content Updates:

• Fresh and Updated Content: Regularly update and refresh content to keep it relevant, accurate, and aligned with the latest information and trends.

9. Transparent and Trustworthy Content:

• Credible Sources and Citations: Support your content with authoritative sources, citations, and references to establish credibility and trustworthiness.

10. Ad Placement Consideration:

• Ad-Friendly Layout: Design your website with a user-friendly layout that allows for well-integrated and non-intrusive ad placements without compromising user experience.

By implementing these strategies, content creators can produce AdSense-friendly content that aligns with AdSense policies, attracts targeted audiences, enhances engagement, and maximizes revenue potential through effective ad monetization.

HOW TO AVOID PROHIBITED CONTENT TYPES

Avoiding prohibited content types is crucial to ensure compliance with AdSense policies and maintain a healthy relationship with the platform. Here are steps to steer clear of prohibited content:

1. Review AdSense Policies:

• Thorough Understanding: Familiarize yourself with AdSense Program Policies, Content Policies, and Webmaster Quality Guidelines. Regularly review policy updates and adhere to their guidelines.

2. Identify Prohibited Content Types:

Explicitly Prohibited Content: Understand and avoid content types explicitly prohibited by AdSense, such as:

• Adult content (pornography, nudity, sexual content)

- Illegal or pirated content

- Content promoting violence, hate speech, discrimination, or illegal activities

- Misleading content or scams

- Copyright-infringing material

3. Content Review and Monitoring:

- Regular Content Audits: Routinely review your content to ensure compliance with AdSense policies. Remove or modify any content that may violate policies.

- User-Generated Content (UGC): If your platform allows user-generated content, implement moderation and monitoring systems to filter out prohibited content.

4. Use Safe Content Topics:

Safe and Neutral Topics: Opt for content that falls within safe and neutral categories:

- Educational content

- How-to guides and tutorials

- Technology-related topics

- Health and wellness (following medical guidelines)

• Lifestyle, travel, and entertainment (non-offensive)

5. Quality and Accuracy:

• Credible Sources: Ensure content accuracy by citing credible sources, avoiding misinformation or misleading claims.

• Fact-Checking: Double-check facts and information before publishing to maintain accuracy and credibility.

6. Brand-Safe Environment:

• Content Sensitivity: Avoid controversial or sensitive topics that might be detrimental to advertisers' brand safety.

7. Monitor User Engagement:

• User Comments and Interactions: Regularly monitor and moderate user comments and interactions to prevent the spread of prohibited content.

8. Compliance Tools and Resources:

• AdSense Compliance Resources: Utilize AdSense's compliance resources, forums, and support to clarify any uncertainties regarding content compliance.

9. Stay Updated:

• Policy Changes and Updates: Stay informed about policy changes and updates issued by AdSense to ensure ongoing compliance with the latest guidelines.

10. Seek Legal Advice if Unsure:

• Legal Counsel: When in doubt about specific content types, seek legal advice to ensure compliance with AdSense policies and applicable laws.

By proactively monitoring, reviewing, and adhering to AdSense policies, content creators can mitigate the risk of hosting prohibited content types and maintain a safe and compliant environment for their users and advertisers, fostering a healthy and profitable relationship with AdSense.

HOW TO ENSURE CONTENT QUALITY

Ensuring content quality is crucial for engaging users, attracting traffic, and complying with AdSense policies. Here are steps to maintain high-quality content:

1. Understand Audience Needs:

• Audience Research: Conduct thorough audience research to understand their interests, preferences, and pain points.

• User Feedback: Gather feedback through surveys, comments, or social media to understand what content resonates with your audience.

2. Content Planning and Strategy:

• Clear Objectives: Define clear goals and objectives for your content strategy aligned with audience needs.

• Content Calendar: Create a content calendar outlining topics, publishing schedules, and planned updates to maintain consistency.

3. Valuable and Relevant Content:

• Solve Problems: Address user queries, provide solutions, and offer valuable information to meet audience needs.

• Originality: Produce original, unique, and insightful content that stands out in your niche.

4. Comprehensive and In-Depth Information:

• Thorough Research: Conduct extensive research to provide in-depth and accurate information on the chosen topics.

• Comprehensive Coverage: Cover topics comprehensively, including various aspects or angles to add depth to your content.

5. Engaging Writing Style:

• Clear and Concise: Write in a clear, easy-to-understand language, avoiding jargon, and complex sentences.

- Engage with Multimedia: Use images, infographics, videos, and interactive elements to make your content visually appealing and engaging.

6. SEO-Friendly Content:

- Keyword Optimization: Incorporate relevant keywords naturally into your content to enhance visibility without compromising readability.

- Meta Tags and Descriptions: Optimize meta tags, titles, and descriptions for search engine visibility.

7. Proper Formatting and Structure:

- Headings and Subheadings: Use clear and descriptive headings and subheadings to organize content logically.

- Bullet Points and Lists: Use bullet points, lists, and formatting to make content scannable and easier to read.

8. Regular Updates and Maintenance:

- Content Refresh: Update and refresh older content periodically to keep it relevant and up-to-date.

- Remove Outdated Content: Remove outdated or irrelevant content that no longer serves its purpose.

9. Credible Sources and References:

• Cite Sources: Support your content with references, data, or citations from reputable and authoritative sources to enhance credibility.

10. User Experience (UX):

• Mobile Optimization: Ensure your content is responsive and optimized for various devices, enhancing user experience.

• Fast Loading Speed: Optimize your website for speed to provide a seamless browsing experience.

By implementing these strategies, content creators can maintain high-quality content that resonates with their audience, attracts traffic, and complies with AdSense policies, fostering a conducive environment for revenue generation.

WHAT ACTIONS CAN RESULT IN POLICY VIOLATIONS

Policy violations on AdSense can occur due to various actions or content that do not align with AdSense Program Policies and Webmaster Quality Guidelines. Here are actions that can result in policy violations:

1. Invalid Clicks and Impressions:

• Click Fraud: Clicking on your ads or encouraging others to click on ads artificially to generate revenue is strictly prohibited.

• Engagement in Click Exchanges: Participating in click exchange programs or clicking on other publishers' ads in exchange for clicks on your own.

2. Content Violations:

• Prohibited Content: Hosting content that violates AdSense content policies, including adult content, copyrighted material, violent or hate speech, illegal content, etc.

• Misleading Content: Publishing misleading or deceptive content that aims to trick users or misrepresent information.

3. Ad Implementation:

• Placing Ads on Unsupported Platforms: Displaying AdSense ads on websites or platforms that are not compliant with AdSense program policies.

• Manipulative Ad Placement: Implementing ads in a way that encourages accidental clicks (e.g., placing ads too close to navigational elements).

4. Ad Behavior:

• Ad Behavior Manipulation: Altering ad code, modifying ad behavior, or using software to generate automated clicks or impressions.

• Encouraging Clicks: Encouraging users to click on ads (explicitly or implicitly) through misleading incentives, deceptive language, or call-to-action.

5. Website and Traffic Quality:

• Low-Quality Traffic: Generating or purchasing low-quality traffic or incentivizing users to visit your website to increase ad impressions.

• Low-Quality Website: Maintaining websites with poor user experience, including excessive ads, irrelevant content, or broken elements.

6. Violation of Google Webmaster Guidelines:

• SEO Manipulation: Employing deceptive SEO practices that violate Google's Webmaster Guidelines, such as keyword stuffing, cloaking, or hidden text.

• Malware or Harmful Behavior: Hosting malware, phishing, or engaging in harmful behaviors that compromise user safety.

7. Copyright Infringement:

• Using Copyrighted Material Without Permission: Publishing content that infringes upon copyrights, trademarks, or intellectual property rights.

8. Violation of Other Google Policies:

• Violation of Other Google Policies: Engaging in actions that breach other Google policies (e.g., Google Ads, Google Search Console) and affect AdSense compliance.

9. Failure to Comply with Regional Laws:

• Non-compliance with Regional Laws: Failing to adhere to local or regional laws and regulations that impact online content and advertising practices.

10. Repeated Policy Violations:

• Repeated Violations: Continuously violating AdSense policies despite warnings or previous violations, leading to account suspension or termination.

AdSense policies are comprehensive, and it's essential to adhere to them to maintain a healthy and compliant ad revenue stream. Regularly reviewing AdSense policies and guidelines can help prevent unintentional violations and ensure sustained adherence to the program's regulations.

Preventing accidental violations of AdSense policies is crucial for maintaining a healthy and compliant monetization strategy. Here are strategies to help prevent accidental policy violations:

1. Familiarize Yourself with Policies:

• Thorough Understanding: Read and understand AdSense Program Policies, Content Policies, and Webmaster Quality Guidelines thoroughly.

• Regular Updates: Stay updated with policy changes and updates released by AdSense to ensure ongoing compliance.

2. Educate Team Members:

• Team Training: Educate your content creators, editors, and website administrators about AdSense policies and guidelines to prevent inadvertent violations.

3. Ad Placement and Implementation:

• Use Authorized Platforms: Ensure that AdSense ads are displayed only on approved and compliant websites or platforms.

• Ad Placement Best Practices: Follow AdSense ad placement policies and guidelines, avoiding manipulative or accidental clicks.

4. Content Quality and Compliance:

• Content Review Process: Implement a content review process to assess content quality and compliance with AdSense policies before publishing.

• Policy Checklists: Create internal checklists or guidelines based on AdSense policies to ensure content meets compliance standards.

5. Monitor User-Generated Content (UGC):

• Moderation Systems: Employ moderation systems for user-generated content (comments, forums) to filter out inappropriate or policy-violating content.

• User Guidelines: Set clear guidelines for users to adhere to when contributing content to your platform.

6. Regular Audits and Checks:

• Periodic Audits: Conduct routine audits of your website or platform to identify and address any potential policy violations promptly.

• Policy Compliance Tools: Utilize tools provided by AdSense or third-party services to scan for policy compliance issues.

7. Communication and Reporting:

• Transparent Communication: Encourage users or visitors to report policy-violating content or suspicious activities to ensure swift action.

8. Stay Informed and Seek Clarification:

• Official Channels for Queries: Use official support channels or forums provided by AdSense for clarifications regarding policy compliance.

• Consultation with Experts: Seek advice from legal experts or consultants when in doubt about specific policy implications.

9. Review Partner Agreements and Contracts:

• Third-Party Partnerships: Review agreements and contracts with third-party partners to ensure they comply with AdSense policies.

10. Proactive Approach:

• Preventive Measures: Take a proactive approach by continuously assessing and updating your content and website to comply with policies.

By implementing these strategies and promoting a culture of compliance within your organization or platform, you can significantly reduce the likelihood of accidental policy violations and maintain a safe and compliant environment for

AdSense monetization. Regular education, monitoring, and adherence to policies are key to preventing unintentional violations.

HOW TO HANDLE ACCOUNT SUSPENSION

Handling an account suspension on AdSense can be a challenging situation. If your AdSense account gets suspended, here are steps you can take to address it:

1. Review Suspension Notification:

• Understand the Reason: Carefully read the suspension notification provided by AdSense to understand the reason(s) for the suspension.

2. Evaluate Violations:

• Review Policy Violations: Identify the specific policy violations or issues that led to the account suspension.

• Assess the Severity: Determine the severity of the violations and whether they were accidental or deliberate.

3. Correct Issues:

Address Policy Violations: Take immediate action to rectify the violations identified by AdSense. This might involve:

• Removing or modifying content that violates policies.

• Adjusting ad placements or implementation that breached guidelines.

• Resolving any technical issues or compliance concerns.

4. Contact AdSense Support:

• Appeal Process: If you believe the suspension was a mistake or if you have rectified the issues, submit an appeal through the AdSense account. The appeal process typically involves explaining the steps taken to resolve the issues and requesting a review.

• Provide Documentation: If possible, provide any relevant documentation or evidence supporting your appeal to demonstrate compliance.

5. Follow-Up and Persistence:

• Follow-Up Communication: Be persistent but polite in your communications with AdSense support. Follow up on your appeal if you don't receive a response within a reasonable timeframe.

• Clarification and Compliance: Request clarification if needed and ensure full compliance with AdSense policies moving forward.

6. Prevent Recurrence:

• Implement Preventive Measures: Put in place preventive measures to avoid similar policy violations in the future. This might involve stricter content reviews, better ad implementation practices, or staff training on policies.

7. Explore Alternatives:

• Consider Alternatives: While waiting for the resolution of the suspension, explore alternative monetization methods to mitigate the impact on revenue.

8. Patience and Persistence:

• Be Patient: Resolution of account suspensions might take time. Maintain patience during the review process.

• Persist with Compliance: Continue adhering to policies and guidelines even after the suspension is lifted to prevent further issues.

9. Seek Professional Advice:

• Consult Legal Counsel: If needed, seek legal advice or guidance from experts specializing in digital advertising and compliance issues.

10. Learn and Adapt:

• Take Lessons: Use the suspension as a learning opportunity to better understand AdSense policies and guidelines, ensuring ongoing compliance.

Remember that each situation may vary, and AdSense support will assess your case individually. It's essential to be transparent, cooperative, and committed to resolving the issues identified to have the best chance of reinstating your AdSense account.

HOW TO HANDLE POLICY WARNINGS

Handling policy warnings on AdSense requires prompt action and adherence to policies to prevent further issues. Here's a step-by-step guide to managing policy warnings:

1. Understand the Warning:

• Review Notification: Carefully read and understand the policy warning issued by AdSense. Identify the specific policy or content issues highlighted in the warning.

2. Address Policy Violations:

• Immediate Action: Take immediate steps to rectify the policy violations identified in the warning.

• Modify or remove content that violates policies.

• Adjust ad placements or implementation to comply with guidelines.

• Resolve any technical or compliance issues mentioned.

3. Investigate the Root Cause:

• Identify Causes: Assess the reasons behind the policy warning. Determine whether the violations were accidental or resulted from deliberate actions.

4. Ensure Compliance:

• Policy Adherence: Ensure full compliance with AdSense policies moving forward. Review all content, ad placements, and website elements to ensure they align with guidelines.

5. Appeal or Seek Clarification:

• Submit an Appeal (if applicable): If you believe the warning was issued in error or after rectifying the issues, consider appealing through the AdSense account. Provide a clear explanation of actions taken and request a review.

• Seek Clarification: If unsure about the warning or need clarification on specific policy aspects, reach out to AdSense support for guidance.

6. Prevent Recurrence:

Implement Preventive Measures: Put measures in place to prevent similar policy violations in the future:

• Strengthen content review processes.

• Train staff or content creators on AdSense policies.

• Regularly monitor and audit content for compliance.

7. Monitor Account Health:

• Regular Checks: Periodically review your account status and notifications to ensure ongoing compliance and address any potential issues promptly.

8. Learn and Adapt:

• Learn from Mistakes: Use the warning as an opportunity to understand AdSense policies better and adapt practices to avoid future violations.

9. Be Proactive and Patient:

• Proactive Approach: Be proactive in adhering to policies and guidelines to prevent future warnings or issues.

• Patience in Resolution: Resolution of policy warnings might take time. Be patient during the review process.

10. Seek Assistance if Needed:

• Consult Experts: If facing challenges in resolving policy issues, consider seeking advice or guidance from professionals specializing in digital advertising compliance.

Handling policy warnings requires diligence, swift action, and a commitment to maintaining compliance with AdSense policies. By promptly addressing issues, implementing preventive measures, and demonstrating commitment to policy compliance, you can mitigate the impact of warnings and ensure a healthier and compliant AdSense account.

CHAPTER SIX

KEY PERFORMANCE METRICS AND THEIR IMPLICATIONS

Key performance metrics in the context of online advertising, particularly concerning AdSense, provide insights into various aspects of ad performance, website traffic, user engagement, and revenue generation. Here are some key metrics and their implications:

1. RPM (Revenue per Thousand Impressions):

• Implication: RPM measures the estimated earnings generated for every thousand ad impressions served. A higher RPM signifies better revenue generation potential, indicating more effective monetization strategies or higher-paying ads.

2. CTR (Click-Through Rate):

• Implication: CTR represents the percentage of ad clicks compared to the total number of ad impressions. A higher CTR typically indicates more engaging ad content or placements, potentially leading to increased ad revenue.

3. eCPM (Effective Cost Per Mille):

• Implication: eCPM measures the estimated earnings per thousand impressions, regardless of the pricing model. A higher eCPM suggests more efficient monetization strategies and potentially higher revenue from ad impressions.

4. Fill Rate:

• Implication: Fill rate measures the percentage of ad inventory that is successfully filled with ads. A higher fill rate signifies better utilization of ad space, potentially leading to increased revenue opportunities.

5. Conversion Rate:

• Implication: Conversion rate indicates the percentage of users who complete a desired action after clicking on an ad. A higher conversion rate implies more effective ad campaigns or compelling content, contributing to revenue growth.

6. ROI (Return on Investment):

• Implication: ROI measures the profitability of advertising campaigns by comparing revenue against advertising costs. Positive ROI indicates profitable campaigns, while negative ROI suggests inefficient spending.

7. Traffic Sources (Organic, Referral, Direct):

• Implication: Understanding traffic sources helps identify where visitors come from. A higher proportion of organic traffic (from search engines) often indicates good SEO practices, potentially leading to better ad performance and revenue.

8. Page RPM:

• Implication: Page RPM measures the estimated earnings generated per page view. Higher page RPM suggests better revenue generation potential per page, indicating effective ad placements or valuable content.

9. Session Duration and Bounce Rate:

• Implication: Longer session durations and lower bounce rates generally indicate engaging content and a positive user experience, potentially leading to increased ad viewability and revenue.

10. Ad Viewability:

• Implication: Ad viewability measures the percentage of ad impressions that were actually seen by users. Higher ad viewability indicates better opportunities for engagement and potentially increased ad revenue.

11. Ad Impressions and Clicks:

• Implication: Ad impressions show the number of times ads are displayed, while clicks indicate user interactions. Higher impressions may indicate increased ad visibility, while clicks signify engagement, impacting revenue potential.

These key performance metrics provide valuable insights into different aspects of ad performance, user behavior, and revenue generation. Analyzing and optimizing these metrics can help publishers and advertisers make informed decisions to improve ad performance, user experience, and overall revenue.

HOW TO ANALYZE ADSENSE PERFORMANCE METRICS

Analyzing AdSense performance metrics involves examining various key indicators to assess ad revenue, user engagement, and website performance. Here's a step-by-step guide on how to analyze AdSense performance metrics effectively:

1. Access AdSense Dashboard:

• Login to AdSense Account: Access your AdSense account and navigate to the dashboard or reporting section.

2. Understand and Select Metrics:

• Identify Key Metrics: Review available metrics like RPM, CTR, eCPM, ad impressions, clicks, etc.

• Select Timeframe: Choose a specific timeframe for analysis (daily, weekly, monthly) to assess trends and performance changes.

3. Evaluate Revenue Metrics:

• RPM (Revenue per Thousand Impressions): Check RPM to assess earnings generated per thousand ad impressions. Higher RPM indicates better revenue potential.

• eCPM (Effective Cost Per Mille): Analyze eCPM to evaluate earnings per thousand impressions across different ad formats or channels.

4. Assess User Engagement:

• CTR (Click-Through Rate): Examine CTR to gauge user engagement with ads. Higher CTR signifies more effective ad engagement.

• Ad Impressions and Clicks: Analyze the number of ad impressions and clicks to understand ad viewability and user interactions.

5. Review Traffic and Audience Data:

• Traffic Sources: Evaluate traffic sources (organic, referral, direct) to understand where visitors are coming from. Identify high-performing traffic sources.

• Geographical Data: Review geographic data to determine regions contributing the most to ad revenue.

6. Evaluate Ad Placement and Performance:

• Ad Units and Sizes: Analyze performance based on different ad units and sizes. Identify which formats or placements generate better revenue.

• Ad Placement: Assess the impact of ad placements on user engagement and revenue. Optimize placements for higher viewability and engagement.

7. Monitor Website Performance Metrics:

• Page Views and Sessions: Examine page views, sessions, and session duration to understand user behavior and content engagement.

• Bounce Rate: Evaluate bounce rate to assess how engaging your content is. Lower bounce rates often indicate more engaging content.

8. Identify Trends and Patterns:

• Analyze Trends Over Time: Look for patterns or trends in performance metrics over different timeframes. Identify seasonal or cyclical trends.

9. Set Goals and Optimization:

• Set Performance Goals: Define performance benchmarks based on historical data and set goals for improvement.

• Optimization Strategies: Based on insights, implement optimization strategies such as adjusting ad placements, improving content, or targeting specific audiences.

10. Take Action and Monitor Changes:

• Implement Changes: Apply adjustments based on analysis findings. Test different strategies and monitor their impact on performance metrics.

• Continuous Monitoring: Regularly track and review performance metrics to assess the effectiveness of optimizations and make further adjustments as needed.

By systematically analyzing AdSense performance metrics, identifying trends, and implementing optimization strategies, publishers can enhance ad revenue, improve user engagement, and optimize their overall website performance.

HOW TO INTERPRET REPORTS FOR OPTIMIZATION

Interpreting reports from AdSense or any advertising platform is crucial for optimizing ad performance and revenue. Here's a guide on how to interpret these reports for optimization:

1. Analyze Revenue Metrics:

RPM (Revenue per Thousand Impressions): Higher RPM suggests better revenue potential. Identify pages or ad units with high RPM for optimization opportunities.

eCPM (Effective Cost Per Mille): Analyze eCPM to identify which ad types or placements yield the highest revenue per thousand impressions.

2. Assess Engagement Metrics:

CTR (Click-Through Rate): Higher CTR indicates engaging ad content or placements. Analyze high-CTR ad units for optimization or replicate successful ad formats.

Ad Impressions and Clicks: Evaluate ad impressions and clicks to understand which placements generate more interactions.

3. Review Traffic Sources:

Traffic Channels: Examine sources (organic, referral, direct) contributing to ad revenue. Focus on optimizing traffic sources that generate higher revenue.

4. Understand User Behavior:

Session Duration and Bounce Rate: Longer session durations and lower bounce rates signify engaging content. Optimize content on pages with high bounce rates.

5. Assess Ad Placement and Formats:

Ad Units and Sizes: Analyze performance based on different ad units and sizes. Identify which formats or placements generate better revenue.

Ad Placement: Optimize Ad placement by considering viewability and user experience. Test different positions for better engagement without compromising user experience.

6. Monitor Geographic Performance:

Geographical Data: Identify regions contributing the most to ad revenue. Optimize content or targeting for regions with high engagement.

7. Set Optimization Goals:

Define Objectives: Based on analysis, set specific goals for optimization such as increasing CTR, improving ad viewability, or targeting higher-paying niches.

8. Test and Iterate:

A/B Testing: Conduct experiments with different ad placements, formats, or content variations to understand what works best. Implement changes gradually based on successful tests.

9. Implement Changes and Monitor:

Apply Optimizations: Implement identified optimizations based on insights gained. Track performance after changes to measure their impact.

10. Regularly Review and Adapt:

Continuous Monitoring: Regularly review reports and adjust strategies as trends change. Stay adaptable to market shifts or user behavior changes.

11. Seek Insights Beyond Basic Metrics:

Deep Dive Analysis: Use advanced features or analytics tools provided by AdSense or other platforms for more in-depth insights. Look beyond basic metrics for nuanced optimization.

Interpreting reports involves analyzing various metrics in conjunction to uncover patterns or correlations that guide optimization strategies. It's an ongoing process that requires continuous monitoring, testing, and adapting strategies to maximize ad performance and revenue generation.

HOW TO INTERPRET ANALYTICS FOR OPTIMIZATION

To interpret analytics effectively for optimization, follow these steps to glean actionable insights and enhance performance:

1. Define Objectives:

• Set Goals: Determine specific goals for your website or campaign—whether it's increased traffic, higher engagement, improved conversions, or enhanced ad revenue.

2. Identify Key Metrics:

• Traffic Metrics: Analyze metrics like sessions, users, page views, and new vs. returning visitors to understand website traffic trends.

• Engagement Metrics: Review metrics such as bounce rate, session duration, and pages per session to gauge user engagement.

• Conversion Metrics: If applicable, assess conversion-related metrics like conversion rate, goal completions, or e-commerce transactions.

3. Segment and Compare Data:

• Date Ranges: Compare data over different timeframes (daily, weekly, monthly) to identify trends or seasonal patterns.

• Segments: Utilize segments to dissect data by traffic sources, demographics, or user behaviors, enabling more targeted analysis.

4. Traffic Sources and Behavior:

• Source/Medium: Assess traffic sources (organic, direct, referral, social) to identify high-performing channels. Optimize strategies for channels driving the most valuable traffic.

• Behavior Flow: Understand user navigation patterns through the site to identify popular entry or exit points, optimizing those pages for engagement or conversions.

5. Content Analysis:

• Top Pages: Identify top-performing pages based on page views, time on page, or conversion rates. Optimize content or replicate successful elements from these pages.

• Content Drilldown: Drill down into content categories or specific sections to identify high-performing areas for further investment.

6. User Experience Insights:

• Device Category: Analyze data based on device categories (desktop, mobile, tablet) to optimize for the most used devices.

• Page Load Time: Monitor site speed metrics to ensure a fast and smooth user experience, impacting bounce rates and engagement.

7. Conversion Optimization:

• Conversion Funnels: If tracking conversions, analyze funnel drop-offs to identify bottlenecks and optimize steps leading to conversions.

• Landing Page Performance: Assess the performance of landing pages in terms of bounce rates, time on page, and conversions. Optimize these pages for better results.

8. A/B Testing and Iteration:

• Experimentation: Conduct A/B tests on different elements (CTAs, headlines, layouts) to identify high-performing variants and optimize accordingly.

9. Attribution and ROI:

• Attribution Models: Use different attribution models to understand the impact of various touchpoints on conversions or revenue.

• Return on Investment (ROI): If applicable, analyze campaign-specific ROI to optimize budget allocation towards the most profitable channels.

10. Actionable Insights and Implementation:

• Actionable Insights: Synthesize insights gathered into actionable steps—optimizing content, adjusting marketing strategies, or improving user experience.

• Continuous Optimization: Implement changes based on insights gained and continuously iterate strategies for ongoing optimization.

Interpreting analytics involves digging deeper into data, deriving actionable insights, and applying strategic optimizations. By continuously analyzing metrics and adjusting strategies accordingly, you can optimize your website's performance for better user experience, engagement, and ultimately, greater success.

PAYMENT THRESHOLDS

Payment thresholds in the context of AdSense refer to the minimum earnings a publisher must accrue before becoming eligible for payment. Here's a detailed explanation:

1. Threshold Amount:

Minimum Payment: AdSense has a minimum threshold amount that a publisher needs to reach to receive payment. The threshold is $100 USD for most countries.

2. Payment Cycle:

• Monthly Payouts: Payments are typically issued on a monthly basis if the earnings reach or exceed the payment threshold.

• Payment Timing: AdSense payments are processed around the 21st of each month. However, the actual timing may vary based on the payment method and potential delays.

3. Accumulating Earnings:

• Accrued Earnings: Until a publisher reaches the payment threshold, earnings continue to accrue and carry over to the subsequent month(s).

• Rolling Balance: If the earnings do not reach the threshold in a particular month, they roll over to the following month until the threshold is met.

4. Payment Methods and Preferences:

• Payment Options: AdSense offers various payment methods, including Electronic Funds Transfer (EFT), wire transfer, checks, and more, depending on the country.

• Payment Settings: Publishers can set their preferred payment method and provide necessary details in their AdSense account.

5. Payment Hold or Review:

• Account Verification: In some cases, especially for new accounts or if there are suspicious activities, AdSense might hold payments until the account is verified.

• Payment Review: Payments might be reviewed if there are discrepancies or suspected policy violations before releasing funds.

6. Unpaid Balances:

• Below Threshold: If earnings are below the threshold by the end of the month, the balance carries forward to the next payment period.

7. Payments and Currencies:

• Currency Conversion: AdSense pays in the local currency of the publisher's country, and conversions might be subject to currency exchange rates and potential fees from banks or payment processors.

8. Policy Compliance:

• Adherence to Policies: To receive payments, publishers must adhere to AdSense policies, ensuring compliance with content guidelines and avoiding policy violations.

9. Check Specifics:

• Check the Latest Updates: AdSense policies and payment thresholds might change, so it's essential to check the latest terms and conditions provided by AdSense.

Meeting the payment threshold is crucial for receiving earnings from AdSense. Publishers need to track their earnings regularly and ensure they comply with AdSense policies to receive their payments timely and efficiently.

PAYMENT METHODS

AdSense offers various payment methods through which publishers can receive their earnings. The availability of these methods can vary depending on the country or region. Here's a detailed explanation of some common AdSense payment methods:

1. Electronic Funds Transfer (EFT) / Direct Deposit:

• Overview: EFT, also known as Direct Deposit, transfers funds electronically directly to the publisher's bank account.

• Availability: Widely available in many countries where AdSense operates.

• Process: Publishers provide their bank account details (account number, routing number, etc.) in their AdSense account. AdSense initiates electronic transfers to the specified bank account when payment thresholds are met.

2. Wire Transfer:

• Overview: Wire transfers involve the direct transfer of funds from AdSense to the publisher's bank account via the SWIFT network.

• Availability: Available in countries where EFT might not be an option or for publishers who prefer wire transfers.

• Process: Publishers need to provide their bank account details along with additional information required for international wire transfers (SWIFT code, IBAN, bank address, etc.) in their AdSense account.

3. Checks:

• Overview: AdSense issues payments by mailing physical checks to the publisher's address.

• Availability: Available in countries where electronic payment methods might not be feasible or for publishers who prefer receiving paper checks.

• Process: Publishers need to provide their postal address in their AdSense account. Checks are sent in the mail, and publishers deposit them into their bank accounts.

4. Western Union Quick Cash:

• Overview: Western Union Quick Cash allows publishers to receive AdSense payments via Western Union locations.

• Availability: Available in select countries and regions where Western Union services are accessible.

• Process: Publishers need to set up Western Union as their payment method and provide the required details. Payments can be collected from local Western Union branches using specific details provided by AdSense.

5. PayPal:

• Overview: AdSense payments can also be received via PayPal, an online payment platform.

• Availability: Available in some countries where PayPal is supported.

• Process: Publishers link their PayPal accounts to their AdSense accounts. Payments are transferred electronically to the linked PayPal account when the payment threshold is met.

6. Payment Threshold and Methods:

• Threshold Requirements: Each payment method might have different minimum thresholds that need to be met before AdSense initiates payments.

• Currency Conversion and Fees: Depending on the chosen payment method, currency conversion rates and potential transaction fees might apply, impacting the final payment amount received by the publisher.

Publishers need to select the most suitable payment method available in their region and ensure that their payment details are accurate and up to date in their AdSense account to receive their earnings efficiently and securely.

PAYMENT SCHEDULES

AdSense operates on a specific payment schedule for issuing payments to publishers. Here's a detailed explanation of AdSense payment schedules:

1. Monthly Payment Cycle:

• Payment Frequency: AdSense typically issues payments on a monthly basis.

• Payment Timing: Payments are usually processed around the 21st of each month. However, the actual date may vary slightly due to weekends, holidays, or other factors.

2. Payment Threshold and Holdovers:

• Minimum Payment Threshold: Publishers must reach the minimum payment threshold to receive their earnings. The threshold is generally $100 USD.

• Accumulated Earnings: If a publisher's earnings do not reach the threshold in a particular month, the balance carries over to the next payment period.

3. Payment Hold or Review:

• Account Verification: For new accounts or in cases of suspicious activities, AdSense may hold payments until the account is verified.

• Payment Review: Payments might undergo a review process if there are discrepancies or suspected policy violations before releasing the funds.

4. Payment Methods and Processing Time:

• Processing Time: Once payments are issued, the time it takes for funds to reach the publisher's account varies based on the chosen payment method.

• Electronic Methods: Electronic funds transfer (EFT), wire transfers, PayPal, or other electronic methods typically process payments faster compared to physical checks.

5. Currency and Exchange Rates:

• Local Currency: AdSense pays publishers in the local currency of their country.

• Currency Conversion: Currency conversion rates apply when transferring funds, and the final payment received might differ due to fluctuations in exchange rates or fees from banks/payment processors.

6. Payment Holds or Delays:

• Hold Due to Policy Violations: If there are suspected policy violations or issues with the account, payments might be delayed until the matter is resolved.

• Threshold Not Met: Payments are held if earnings do not meet the minimum threshold. The balance carries forward until the threshold is reached.

7. Payment Notifications:

• Payment Notifications: Publishers receive notifications in their AdSense accounts once payments are issued. Notifications also include details regarding the payment method and amount.

8. Tax Withholding or Reporting:

• Tax Information: Publishers may need to provide tax information to AdSense for proper withholding or reporting, depending on their country's tax regulations.

AdSense's payment schedules are structured to ensure that publishers receive their earnings promptly and securely once the minimum payment threshold is met. Understanding the payment schedule and ensuring compliance with AdSense policies are crucial for receiving payments on time.

STRATEGIES TO INCREASE EARNINGS

Increasing earnings through AdSense involves implementing strategies to optimize ad performance, increase user engagement, and improve overall website revenue. Here are some effective strategies to boost AdSense earnings:

1. Optimize Ad Placement:

• Strategic Placement: Position ads where they are more likely to be seen without compromising user experience. Experiment with placements above the fold, within content, or near navigation bars.

• Responsive Ad Units: Use responsive ad units that adapt to various screen sizes and devices for better visibility.

2. Experiment with Ad Formats:

• Test Different Formats: Try various ad formats (text, display, native, video) to find what works best for your audience. Responsive ad units may also improve performance.

3. Focus on High-Performing Content:

• Content Optimization: Create high-quality, engaging content. Identify and optimize pages or topics that generate more traffic and engagement for increased ad views.

• Keyword Optimization: Use SEO strategies to attract organic traffic. Target relevant keywords to boost visibility and attract more visitors.

4. Improve User Experience:

• Page Load Speed: Ensure fast-loading pages to decrease bounce rates and enhance user experience, leading to more ad views.

• Mobile Optimization: Optimize your site for mobile devices to cater to the growing mobile audience and improve ad visibility.

5. Increase Traffic and Engagement:

• Promotion and Marketing: Promote your content through social media, newsletters, guest blogging, etc., to attract more visitors and increase engagement.

• Encourage Interaction: Encourage users to interact with your content (comments, shares, likes), which can increase time spent on site and ad views.

6. A/B Testing and Optimization:

• Continuous Testing: Experiment with different ad placements, formats, colors, and sizes using A/B testing to identify what resonates best with your audience.

7. Target High-Paying Niches:

• Focus on Niche Content: Concentrate on creating content related to high-paying niches or industries to attract ads with better CPC rates.

8. Monitor Performance Metrics:

• Analyze Reports Regularly: Review AdSense reports to understand what works and what doesn't. Use insights to refine your strategies for better results.

9. Implement AdSense Features:

• Use AdSense Features: Utilize features like Custom Channels, URL Channels, and AdSense Experiments to gain deeper insights into ad performance and optimize accordingly.

10. Comply with Policies:

• Adhere to AdSense Policies: Ensure compliance with AdSense policies to avoid penalties or suspensions that could impact earnings.

By combining these strategies and consistently monitoring performance, publishers can enhance their AdSense earnings by maximizing ad visibility, improving user engagement, and optimizing content to attract a larger audience.

STRATEGIES TO MANAGE PAYMENTS EFFICIENTLY

Managing AdSense payments efficiently involves optimizing processes to receive and handle earnings securely and timely. Here are strategies to manage AdSense payments effectively:

• Keep Details Updated: Ensure your payment information, including banking details, address, and preferred payment method, is accurate and up to date in your AdSense account.

• Focus on Earnings: Work towards reaching the minimum payment threshold ($100 USD in most cases) to trigger regular payouts.

• Select Efficient Method: Choose a payment method that suits your preferences and offers efficient processing and low fees based on your location.

• Regularly Check Notifications: Stay updated with AdSense notifications regarding payment issuance, ensuring you're aware of payment status and details.

• Be Aware of Payment Schedule: Familiarize yourself with the AdSense payment schedule to anticipate payment arrival times and plan accordingly.

• Monitor Performance: Regularly track your earnings, payment history, and any pending balances within your AdSense account dashboard.

• Factor in Exchange Rates: Understand how currency exchange rates impact the final amount received and consider strategies to mitigate potential losses due to fluctuating rates.

• Provide Necessary Tax Details: If required, provide accurate tax information to AdSense to comply with tax regulations in your country or region.

• Use Electronic Payment Methods: Prefer electronic payment methods like Electronic Funds Transfer (EFT) or wire transfers for quicker processing compared to checks.

• Prepare for Potential Delays: Understand that payments might be delayed due to various reasons such as holidays, account reviews, or policy checks by AdSense.

• Adhere to Policies: Avoid policy violations that might lead to payment holds or account suspensions, impacting your earnings.

• Ensure Security: Use secure and trusted banking channels for payments to protect your financial information.

• Maintain Records: Keep records of your earnings, payments, and transactions for accounting and reconciliation purposes.

By following these strategies, publishers can effectively manage their AdSense payments, ensuring timely and secure receipt of earnings while optimizing processes for efficient financial management.

COMMON PROBLEMS CONTENT CREATORS FACE WITH ADSENSE

Content creators using AdSense often encounter various challenges that can impact their revenue and overall experience. Some common problems they face include:

• Violation Issues: Content creators might unknowingly breach AdSense policies, leading to warnings, demonetization, or even account suspension.

• Low Revenue: Some creators struggle to generate significant earnings due to factors such as low traffic, poor ad placements, or low-paying niches.

• Click Fraud: Creators might face issues related to click fraud or invalid clicks, impacting their ad revenue and potentially leading to account issues.

• Threshold Not Met: Difficulty in reaching the payment threshold might delay earnings, especially for creators with lower website traffic or engagement.

• Low CTR or RPM: Creators may face challenges in optimizing ad performance, leading to low click-through rates (CTR) or revenue per thousand impressions (RPM).

• Impact of Ad Blockers: Users employing ad-blocking software can significantly reduce ad impressions, affecting the creator's revenue potential.

• AdSense Policy Changes: Frequent updates or changes in AdSense policies can cause confusion or require adjustments in content creation strategies to comply.

• Poor Website Performance: Suboptimal website speed, mobile responsiveness, or user experience can impact ad views and engagement.

• Limited Traffic: Growing an audience and attracting substantial traffic can be challenging, affecting ad views and earnings.

• Account Reviews: Creators may face payment holds or delayed payments due to account reviews or suspicious activities.

• Competitive Niches: Operating in highly competitive niches or industries might lead to lower ad rates or higher competition for traffic.

• Technical Challenges: Optimizing ad placements, formats, or targeting strategies may pose technical challenges for some creators.

Addressing these challenges often requires a combination of strategies, including understanding AdSense policies, optimizing content and ad placements, focusing on audience growth, maintaining website quality, and keeping abreast of industry changes. It's essential for content creators to continuously adapt and refine their approach to navigate these challenges and maximize their AdSense revenue.

TROUBLESHOOTING STEPS FOR VARIOUS AD-RELATED ISSUES

Troubleshooting ad-related issues in AdSense requires a systematic approach to identify and resolve common problems. Here are steps to troubleshoot various ad-related issues:

1. Low Ad Revenue or Earnings:

• Check Ad Performance Metrics: Analyze metrics like RPM, CTR, and ad viewability to identify underperforming ad units or placements.

• Optimize Ad Placements: Experiment with different ad positions, formats, and sizes. Ensure ads are visible without hindering user experience.

• Improve Content Quality: Enhance content relevance and quality to attract more visitors and potentially increase ad views.

2. Policy Violations or Account Issues:

• Review AdSense Policies: Ensure compliance with AdSense policies to avoid violations that can lead to warnings, demonetization, or account suspension.

• Check Account Health: Monitor account notifications and review the AdSense Policy Center for any flagged issues.

3. Ad Blocking Problems:

• Use Anti-Ad Blocking Solutions: Implement anti-ad blocking measures or engage with users to whitelist your site to combat ad blockers.

4. Invalid Clicks or Click Fraud:

• Monitor Click Activity: Regularly review your reports for suspicious click patterns or unusual activity that might indicate click fraud.

• Implement Click Protection Measures: Utilize AdSense's built-in click protection features to prevent invalid clicks.

5. Ad Display Issues:

• Check Ad Code Integration: Ensure ad code implementation on your website is correct and properly integrated into the HTML structure.

• Inspect Website Compatibility: Verify that ads display correctly across various devices and browsers to ensure optimal visibility.

6. Slow Loading Ads:

• Optimize Website Speed: Improve page load times by optimizing images, reducing scripts, and utilizing caching techniques to enhance ad loading speed.

• Review Ad Network Performance: If using multiple ad networks, analyze if any specific network is causing delays and consider adjustments.

7. Payment Problems:

• Review Payment Details: Check payment information in your AdSense account to ensure accuracy and update if necessary.

• Meet Payment Threshold: Ensure earnings reach the minimum threshold for payment eligibility and monitor payment notifications.

8. Ad Formats and Sizes:

• Test Different Formats: Experiment with various ad formats (text, display, native, video) and sizes using A/B testing to determine what works best for your audience.

• Use Responsive Ad Units: Implement responsive ad units that adapt to different screen sizes for better user experience.

9. Lack of Targeted Ads:

• Improve Content Relevance: Create content focused on specific topics or keywords to attract more targeted ads relevant to your audience.

• Use Custom Channels: Utilize AdSense features like Custom Channels to provide advertisers with more information about your content for better targeting.

10. Technical Support:

• Reach Out for Assistance: If issues persist, contact AdSense support for guidance and assistance in resolving complex or persistent problems.

Regularly monitoring ad performance, staying updated on AdSense policies, and making data-driven optimizations can significantly help in troubleshooting ad-related issues and improving overall performance.

HOW TO IMPLEMENT THE GUIDE'S STRATEGIES AND TIPS

Implementing strategies and tips outlined in a comprehensive AdSense guide involves a step-by-step approach and practical execution. Here's how you can implement these strategies effectively:

• Thoroughly Read the Guide: Familiarize yourself with the entire guide, paying attention to specific sections relevant to your goals or areas needing improvement.

• Define Objectives: Identify specific goals you aim to achieve by implementing strategies from the guide — such as increasing ad revenue, improving user engagement, or optimizing ad placements.

• Select Key Strategies: Determine which strategies from the guide align best with your goals and resources. Focus on a few key areas to start with.

• Create an Action Plan: Develop a structured plan outlining the steps needed to implement each strategy effectively.

• Experiment with Ad Placements: Test different ad placements on your website or blog. Monitor performance metrics and adjust placements based on user engagement and ad performance.

• Test Ad Formats and Sizes: A/B test various ad formats and sizes to identify which ones perform best in terms of CTR, user engagement, and revenue generation.

• Optimize Content Quality: Enhance your content by making it more engaging, informative, and relevant to your target audience. Use SEO techniques to improve visibility.

• Improve Website Performance: Enhance site speed, mobile responsiveness, and overall user experience to encourage more ad views and engagement.

• Promote Your Content: Utilize social media, SEO, email marketing, and other channels to attract more visitors and grow your audience.

• Review AdSense Policies: Ensure strict adherence to AdSense policies to avoid violations that could impact your account health and revenue.

• Regular Monitoring: Keep a close eye on ad performance metrics, user engagement, and revenue trends using AdSense reports.

• Iterative Optimization: Continuously optimize based on the insights gained. Use A/B testing and experimentation to refine strategies for better results.

• Utilize AdSense Resources: Refer to AdSense Help Center, forums, and other resources provided by Google for additional guidance and support.

- Measure Success: Track progress towards your goals by regularly assessing performance metrics and revenue growth.

- Adapt Strategies: Adjust your strategies based on the performance data to continuously improve your ad monetization efforts.

By systematically implementing the strategies outlined in the guide, monitoring their impact, and making data-driven adjustments, you can effectively optimize your AdSense usage and improve revenue generation while ensuring a positive user experience on your website or platform.

FAQS WITH CLEAR, CONCISE ANSWERS.

Here is a compilation of FAQs related to AdSense along with clear and concise answers:

1. What is Google AdSense?

- Answer: Google AdSense is an advertising program run by Google that allows website owners or publishers to monetize their online content by displaying targeted ads. Publishers earn revenue based on clicks or impressions of these ads.

2. How does AdSense work?

- Answer: AdSense works by placing targeted ads on participating websites. Advertisers bid to display their ads through Google's ad auction. When users visit a site with

AdSense ads and interact with them (clicks or views), the publisher earns a portion of the ad revenue.

3. What are the eligibility requirements for AdSense?

• Answer: Publishers need to have original content, be at least 18 years old, comply with AdSense policies, and have a website that meets Google's quality guidelines to be eligible for AdSense.

4. How do I sign up for AdSense?

• Answer: To sign up for AdSense, visit the AdSense website, create an account, provide your website URL, and follow the steps to submit your application. Upon approval, you can generate ad codes to display on your site.

5. What are the different ad formats supported by AdSense?

• Answer: AdSense supports various ad formats, including display ads, text ads, native ads, video ads, and link units, which can be customized in different sizes and styles.

6. How do I get paid through AdSense?

• Answer: AdSense pays publishers once they reach the minimum payment threshold ($100 USD in most cases) via payment methods such as Electronic Funds Transfer (EFT), wire transfer, checks, or other available options.

7. Why was my AdSense application rejected?

• Answer: AdSense may reject applications due to insufficient content, policy violations, non-compliance with guidelines, or issues with website quality, among other reasons.

8. What should I do if my AdSense account is suspended?

• Answer: If your AdSense account is suspended, review the reason provided in the notification. Address the issues, rectify policy violations, and follow the appeal process outlined by Google to reinstate your account.

9. How can I optimize my AdSense earnings?

• Answer: Optimize your earnings by improving ad placements, creating high-quality content, increasing website traffic, experimenting with ad formats, and focusing on user experience.

10. What is RPM in AdSense?

• Answer: RPM (Revenue per Mille) is a metric in AdSense that represents the estimated earnings a publisher generates per thousand impressions (page views) on their site.

11. Can I use AdSense with other ad networks?

• Answer: Yes, you can use AdSense with other ad networks, but it's important to comply with policies regarding ad placement and avoid violating Google's terms of service.

12. How can I troubleshoot low ad revenue or ad display issues?

• Answer: To troubleshoot low ad revenue, review ad placements, optimize content, check for policy compliance, monitor ad performance metrics, and explore different ad formats or sizes.

CONCLUSION

In conclusion, Google AdSense stands as a powerful platform for content creators seeking to monetize their online presence. Through strategic ad placements and a deep understanding of audience engagement, AdSense empowers creators to convert their passion and content into a sustainable revenue stream.

As content creation continues to evolve, AdSense remains a vital tool, offering a seamless integration of relevant ads that complement rather than interrupt the user experience. However, success with AdSense demands more than just ad placements. It necessitates a keen eye for optimization, a commitment to quality content, and a dedication to adhere to policies and guidelines.

For content creators, embracing AdSense isn't solely about monetization; it's about fostering a symbiotic relationship between content, audience, and advertisements. By continuously refining strategies, experimenting with formats, and prioritizing user experience, creators can unlock the full potential of AdSense while nurturing a thriving online community.

The journey with AdSense is not without its challenges — policy compliance, revenue fluctuations, or user engagement hurdles — but it's the relentless pursuit of improvement and the ability to adapt that define a successful partnership with AdSense.

As the digital landscape evolves, content creators navigating the realms of AdSense must remain vigilant, innovative, and in tune with their audience's needs. Through this synergy, AdSense serves as not just a revenue-generating platform but a catalyst for creativity, innovation, and sustainable growth in the ever-expanding realm of online content creation.